KB084573

TOEFL® MAP

MAP

New TOEFL® Edition

Writing

Basic

DARAKWON

TOEFL® MAP

MAP *New TOEFL® Edition*

Writing Basic

Publisher Chung Kyudo
Editors Zong Ziin, Cho Sangik
Authors Jonathan S. McClelland, Shane Spivey
Proofreader Michael A. Putlack
Designers Park Narae, Yoon Hyunju

First published in June 2022
By Darakwon, Inc.
Darakwon Bldg., 211, Munbal-ro, Paju-si, Gyeonggi-do 10881
Republic of Korea
Tel: 82-2-736-2031 (Ext. 250)
Fax: 82-2-732-2037

ISBN 978-89-277-8029-8 14740
978-89-277-8025-0 14740 (set)

www.darakwon.co.kr

Photo Credits
Shutterstock.com

Components Main Book / Scripts and Answer Key
8 7 6 5 4 3 2   24 25 26 27 28

Introduction

Studying for the TOEFL® iBT is no easy task and is not one that is to be undertaken lightly. It requires a great deal of effort as well as dedication on the part of the student. It is our hope that, by using *TOEFL® Map Writing Basic* as either a textbook or a study guide, the task of studying for the TOEFL® iBT will become somewhat easier for the student and less of a burden.

Students who wish to excel on the TOEFL® iBT must attain a solid grasp of the four important skills in the English language: reading, listening, speaking, and writing. The Darakwon *TOEFL® Map* series covers all four of these skills in separate books across three different levels. This book, *TOEFL® Map Writing Basic*, covers the writing aspect of the test at the basic level. Students who want to read passages, listen to lectures, learn vocabulary items, and write essays in response to tasks that appear on the TOEFL® iBT will have their wishes granted by using this book.

TOEFL® Map Writing Basic has been designed for use in both a classroom setting and as a study guide for individual learners. For this reason, it offers a comprehensive overview of the TOEFL® iBT Writing section. In Part A, the Integrated and Independent Tasks of the TOEFL® iBT Writing section are explained, and writing tips to assist students are included. In Part B, learners have the opportunity to build their background knowledge by studying reading passages, lectures, and writing tasks that have appeared on the TOEFL® iBT. In addition, each chapter includes vocabulary word sections that enable learners to understand the words that frequently appear in the TOEFL® iBT Writing section and incorporate them into their writing. Every chapter also features paraphrasing and summarizing exercises and sample response analysis questions to help learners become more adept at analyzing arguments made in the reading passages and lectures and creating essays in response. Finally, in Part C, students can take two complete TOEFL® iBT practice tests. Each of these tests includes Integrated and Independent Writing Tasks that have appeared on the actual TOEFL® iBT Writing section. When combined, all of these practice exercises help learners prepare themselves to take and, more importantly, excel on the TOEFL® iBT.

TOEFL® Map Writing Basic has a vast amount of information and should prove to be invaluable as a study guide for learners who are preparing for the TOEFL® iBT. However, while this book is comprehensive, it is up to each person to do the actual work. In order for *TOEFL® Map Writing Basic* to be of any use, the individual learner must dedicate himself or herself to studying the information found within its pages. While we have strived to make this book as user friendly and as full of crucial information as possible, ultimately, it is up to each person to make the best of the material in the book. We wish you luck in your study of both English and the TOEFL® iBT, and we hope that you are able to use *TOEFL® Map Writing Basic* to improve your skills in both of them.

Jonathan S. McClelland
Shane Spivey

TABLE OF CONTENTS

How Is This Book Different?

TOEFL® Map Writing Basic is not a typical TOEFL® study book. Of course, it is similar to other TOEFL® books in that it replicates the types of passages and questions you will come across on the test. However, this book differs in its focus: critical thinking. *TOEFL® Map Writing Basic* will teach you how to critically analyze the material you will see on the actual writing section of the TOEFL®, so it will give you the skills needed to earn a top score on the test. Here are the standout features of this book:

Critical Analysis

Summarizing and Paraphrasing

To be successful on the writing section of the TOEFL® iBT test, you must be able to summarize and paraphrase information accurately. Therefore, this book includes summary exercises after the reading passage and the lecture. Following these exercises is a paraphrasing practice section. This task requires you to paraphrase words and phrases in the sentences from the summary exercises.

Sample Responses Analysis

One of the best ways to learn is from examples. It is for this reason that each chapter includes a benchmark sample response after the student writing task. These benchmark responses let you see what makes a response strong. They also allow you to understand how to present the material from the reading passage and the lecture.

Intuitive Integrated Note Taking

Tandem Note-Taking for Integrated Writing

TOEFL® Map Writing Basic includes the standard outlining sections after the reading passage and the lecture. But it also includes a unique tandem note-taking section. The tandem note-taking section requires you to complete side-by-side outlines for both the reading passage and the lecture. Having notes for both the reading and the lecture next to each other on the same page will allow you to analyze the relationship between them more quickly, easily, and accurately.

Background Information for Independent Writing

For many students, generating supporting ideas is the most difficult aspect of the Independent Writing Task. This is why this book includes background information for each writing task. Following the reading is a set of comprehension questions. By reading the background information, you will have a better understanding of how to answer the Independent Writing Task.

Vocabulary Building

Vocabulary Boxes

To earn a high score on the TOEFL® iBT, a strong vocabulary is essential. For this reason, each chapter in TOEFL® Map Writing Basic includes two vocabulary boxes in the Integrated Writing Section. Each vocabulary box includes six to ten words and gives the part of speech, the definition, and the use in context for each word.
Following this is a short exercise using the vocabulary words to complete sentences. This will enable you to identify these words successfully when they appear on the actual TOEFL® iBT while allowing you to make your writing more vivid and succinct.

How to Use
This Book

TOEFL® Map Writing Basic is designed for use either as a textbook in a classroom or in a TOEFL® iBT preparation course. It can also be used as a study guide for individuals who are studying for the TOEFL® iBT on their own. *TOEFL® Map Writing Basic* has been divided into three sections: Part A, Part B, and Part C. All three sections offer information that is important to learners preparing for the TOEFL® iBT. Part A is divided into 3 chapters that introduce the Writing section, the Integrated Writing Task, and the Independent Writing Task. Part B is divided into 8 chapters. Each chapter includes passages and questions similar to those that have appeared on the TOEFL® iBT. Part C has 2 actual tests consisting of Integrated and Independent Writing Tasks that resemble those appearing on the TOEFL® iBT.

Part A Understanding Writing Question Types

This section is designed to explain the TOEFL® iBT Writing section. It is divided into 3 chapters. The first chapter provides an overview of the Writing section. It goes over the general requirements of the Integrated and Independent Writing Tasks. It also features an explanation of how to organize essays and includes an exercise for you to complete. The second chapter breaks down the Integrated Writing Task. It provides a detailed explanation of the question types and the writing requirements. It includes a sample Integrated Writing reading passage, lecture, and question, too. This chapter also provides writing tips and explains the note-taking and sample response sections included throughout the book. The final chapter breaks down the Independent Writing Task. It provides a detailed explanation of the question types and writing requirements for this task. This chapter includes writing tips and emphasizes developing organizational skills when writing. It also includes a sample Independent Writing Task question.

Part B Building Knowledge & Skills for the Writing Test

The purpose of this section is to introduce passages on various topics that have appeared on the TOEFL® iBT. There are 8 chapters in Part B. Each one includes an Integrated Writing Task and an Independent Writing Task. Every chapter also has vocabulary boxes, critical thinking, and sample response analysis exercises. Each chapter is divided into several parts.

Integrated Writing Task – Reading Passage

This section begins by introducing 6 to 10 new vocabulary words that appear in the reading passage. Following the reading passage is a summarizing exercise designed to help you fully understand the reading passage.

Integrated Writing Task – Lecture

This section is similar to the reading passage section. It introduces 6 to 10 new vocabulary words that are included in the lecture and features note-taking and critical-thinking exercises. Similar to the reading passage section, this section contains a summarizing exercise designed to help you understand the lecture. This will enable you to write a higher-scoring response for the writing task.

Integrated Writing Task – Paraphrasing Exercise

This section includes 5 sentences each from the summarizing exercises for the reading passage and lecture. Beneath each sentence is an incomplete paraphrase of the sentence above. You must complete these by using synonyms and phrases with similar meanings. By doing this, you will understand how to write summarized information in your own words.

Integrated Writing Task – Tandem Note-Taking

This section requires you to briefly summarize the information from the previous two sections in two vertical columns. This arrangement allows you to expand your notes by adding supporting details from the reading passage and lecture while allowing you to better understand the relationship between the two passages.

Integrated Writing Task – Writing Section and Scaffolding

This section includes the question for the Integrated Writing Task and provides space for you to write your response. It also features a writing guide to help you organize your essay as you write. At the end of this section is the scaffolding portion, which includes useful phrases for you to incorporate into your response.

Integrated Writing Task – Sample Response

This section features a well-written response to the writing task given in the previous section. You can see how to improve your own response by analyzing the organizational techniques, the transitions, and the vocabulary used in the strong response.

Independent Writing Task – Background

This section begins by presenting the Independent Writing Task question for the chapter. Following this is background information about the question. It presents ideas and supporting arguments for both sides of the given task. A short reading comprehension exercise about the background information concludes this section.

Independent Writing Task – Selecting and Generating Ideas

This section contains summarized and paraphrased information from the background reading. The selecting ideas exercise requires you to determine which ideas relate to which argument. You must then complete the generating ideas exercise. This requires you to complete paraphrased sentences from the selecting ideas exercise.

Independent Writing Task – Planning

This section consists of a detailed note-taking exercise that requires you to write your thesis statement, supporting ideas, and examples.

Independent Writing Task – Writing Section and Scaffolding

This section reintroduces the writing task for the chapter and provides space for you to write your response. It also features a writing guide to help you organize your essay as you write. At the end of this section is the scaffolding portion, which includes useful phrases for you to incorporate into your essay.

Independent Writing Task – Sample Response

This section features a well-written response to the writing task given in the previous section. You can see how to improve your own response by analyzing the organization, the transitions, the main ideas, and the examples used in the strong response.

Part C Experiencing the TOEFL iBT Actual Tests

This section contains 2 complete TOEFL® iBT Writing section tests. The purpose of this section is to let you experience the actual Writing section and to see if you can apply the skills you have learned in the course of studying *TOEFL® Map Writing Basic*.

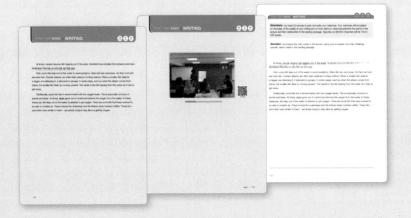

Part A

Understanding Writing Question Types

Organizing Information

The writing section is the last part of the TOEFL® test. It has two parts. The first part is the Integrated Writing Task. This task lasts 20 minutes. The second part is the Independent Writing Task. This part lasts 30 minutes. In the Integrated Writing Task, students need to explain how a short reading passage and a lecture are related. In the Independent Writing Task, test takers must explain their opinions about a given situation.

The writing section tests students on their ability to organize information clearly. The responses do not have to be creative. They just need to answer the questions clearly. For both tasks, the essays should be organized in the following way:

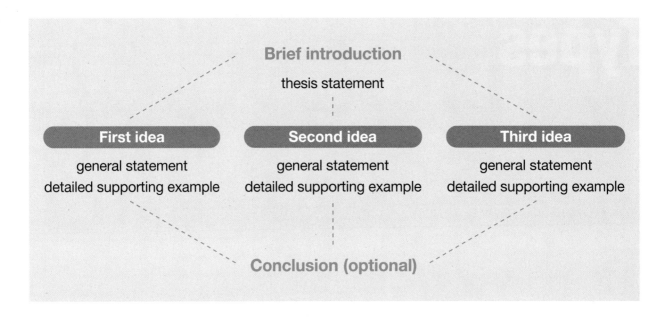

Brief introduction

thesis statement

First idea	**Second idea**	**Third idea**
general statement	general statement	general statement
detailed supporting example	detailed supporting example	detailed supporting example

Conclusion (optional)

An essay that uses this basic organization is likely earn a high score. Test takers can use detailed supporting examples to improve their scores. Strong supporting examples and clear details are needed to earn a top score.

Please note that the TOEFL® evaluators understand that test takers do not have much time to plan their essays. The evaluators also know that test takers are not native English speakers. They do not expect test takers to write perfect essays. They are simply looking to see that test takers can write their ideas clearly. An essay with mistakes can still earn a top score.

Information Organization Exercise

Each of the following boxes contains ideas for an essay. Organize the information so that it fits logically into the outlines provided below.

1
- Moreover, I have less work to do during summer.
- I enjoy going to the beach with my family.
- I am on vacation during summer.
- For one, summer has the best weather.
- My favorite season is summer.

▪ **Thesis Statement** ....

▪ **First Supporting Argument** ....

  Detailed Supporting Example ....

▪ **Second Supporting Argument** ....

  Detailed Supporting Example ....

2
- The first reason is that playing games is not healthy.
- Children should not be allowed to play video games.
- Gamers spend less time talking with other people.
- Children eat junk food and gain weight.
- On top of this, games also do not allow children to develop social skills.

▪ **Thesis Statement** ....

▪ **First Supporting Argument** ....

  Detailed Supporting Example ....

▪ **Second Supporting Argument** ....

  Detailed Supporting Example ....

Explanation of the Integrated Writing Task

The Integrated Writing Task has three parts. The first part is a reading passage. The passage is between 230 and 300 words long. Test takers have three minutes to read the passage. The next part is a lecture. The lecture either supports or goes against the reading. Finally, test takers have 20 minutes to write their essays. The essays should be between 150 and 225 words in length. During this time, test takers can see the reading passage. Remember that test takers do not have to provide any new ideas in their essays. Instead, they must summarize the lecture and explain how it relates to the reading passage. To do this, they should give examples from both the lecture and the reading passage.

Integrated Writing Task Wording

There are four possible writing tasks that may be given. All of them require test takers to summarize the lecture and to explain how it either supports or contradicts the reading passage.

The listening lecture may challenge or contradict the reading passage. If it does this, then the task will be presented in one of the following ways:

▶ Summarize the points made in the lecture, being sure to explain how they cast doubt on specific points made in the reading passage.

▶ Summarize the points made in the lecture, being sure to explain how they challenge specific claims/arguments made in the reading passage.

   cf. *These questions account for almost all of the questions that have been asked on the TOEFL® iBT so far.*

The listening lecture may also answer problems raised in the reading passage. If it does this, then the task will be presented in the following way:

▶ Summarize the points made in the lecture, being sure to specifically explain how they answer the problems raised in the reading passage.

Lastly, the listening lecture may support or strengthen the reading passage. If it does this, then the task will be presented in the following way:

▶ Summarize the points made in the lecture, being sure to specifically explain how they support the explanations in the reading passage.

Writing Tips for the Integrated Writing Task

- Take notes on all of the main ideas from the reading passage and the lecture. Do not try to write everything. However, try to include the supporting arguments and the examples for each idea from both the reading passage and the lecture. Be sure to put your notes in two columns.

- Take one minute to organize your ideas before you begin writing. Look over your notes as you write.

- Focus primarily on summarizing the lecture in your response. Be sure to include all of the main ideas and the examples from the lecture. Do not give your opinion about the topic.

- Begin each paragraph with clear, simple transitions.

- Manage your time wisely. Try to spend no more than five minutes writing each paragraph.

- Use the last one to three minutes to proofread your response. Correct errors as needed.

Sample Integrated Writing Task

⊘ Reading Passage

On the Integrated Writing Task, a reading passage like the one below will be given to you first. You will have three minutes to read the passage.

> These days, many people are opposed to using animals in laboratory testing. These people do not understand the importance of animal testing in modern science. Quite simply, modern scientific advancements could not happen without animal testing.
>
> First of all, animal testing improves human life. Animal testing has made many important developments over the past few decades possible. It is especially important for the creation of prescription drugs. In nearly every country in the world, new medicines are first tested on animals. This allows researchers to learn how a drug works. They can also find out what dangerous side effects a drug has. Thanks to animal testing, scientists have been able to make new medicines that save lives.
>
> Additionally, animal testing is the most effective way to test products. Scientists must fully understand how a product affects living creatures. Some animals are very good for this kind of testing. The reason is that they are very similar to human beings. One such animal is the chimpanzee. Human beings share over ninety-nine percent of their genetic information with chimpanzees. When a product is tested on a chimpanzee, scientists learn exactly how it would affect a human being. Other ways of testing a product cannot be this accurate. Therefore, researchers must continue animal testing.

Following this, you will listen to a lecture:

⊘ Lecture

Narrator (Male)

Now listen to part of a lecture on the topic you just read about.

01-01

Professor (Male)

I want to move on to another controversial subject. I'm talking, of course, about animal testing. We've already heard the arguments in favor of animal testing. Now, I'd like to give you some reasons why animal testing should be stopped.

For starters, animal testing is just not that helpful. Most of the time, animal testing doesn't produce useful results. For example, one drug company created a medicine to treat depression. The scientists tested the drug on mice with no problems. But when they gave the drug to humans, something terrible happened. All the people became very sick. They had to go to the hospital. From this, we can see that testing drugs on animals doesn't always prove that they are safe for human beings.

Another thing to keep in mind is the alternatives to animal testing. These days, scientists have many other methods to test products. One method is to use human cells for testing. This method has two advantages. First, it doesn't hurt living creatures. Second, it is more accurate because the cells come from human beings. And with today's advanced computers, it is possible to test products by using computer models. With all these alternatives, it seems to me that animal testing is no longer needed.

Once the listening is finished, the reading passage will reappear along with the following directions and the writing task:

⊘ Directions and Writing Task

Directions You have 20 minutes to plan and write your response. Your response will be judged on the basis of the quality of your writing and on how well your response presents the points in the lecture and their relationship to the reading passage. Typically, an effective response will be 150 to 225 words.

Question Summarize the points made in the lecture, being sure to explain how they challenge specific claims made in the reading passage.

At this time, you will have 20 minutes to complete your essay.

Summarizing and Paraphrasing

To do well on the writing portion of the TOEFL®, you must be able to summarize information. This requires you to present the most important ideas from the reading passage and the lecture. The following exercise shows you how to do this successfully.

⊘ Sample Summarizing

The summary table below consists of paraphrased information from the reading passage.

Main Idea The author of the reading passage feels that scientific advancements could not happen without animal testing. The writer gives two reasons to support this argument.

First Supporting Argument First, the author argues that animal testing improves human lives. According to the passage, many important developments have occurred because of animal testing. Animal testing has been especially important in the creation of prescription drugs.

Second Supporting Argument Next, the author explains that animal testing is the most effective way to test products. Some animals, such as the chimpanzee, are very similar to human beings. By testing products on these animals, scientists can learn how they would affect a human being.

Another necessary skill for the TOEFL writing section is paraphrasing. To paraphrase, you must rewrite the ideas from the reading passage and the lecture by using your own words. One way you can do this is by changing the sentence structure. You can also paraphrase by using synonyms in your response.

⊘ Sample Paraphrasing

The following sentences from the reading passage summary can be paraphrased in the following ways.

> **1** The author of the reading passage feels that scientific advancements could not happen without animal testing.
>
> → *In the reading passage, the author argues that animal testing is necessary for important scientific advancements to occur.*
>
> **2** First, the author argues that animal testing improves human lives.
>
> → *The author's first argument is that animal testing makes human lives better.*
>
> **3** Animal testing has been especially important in the creation of prescription drugs.
>
> → *Animal testing has been very useful in making prescription drugs.*
>
> **4** Some animals, such as the chimpanzee, are very similar to human beings.
>
> → *Animals such as the chimpanzee are very much like human beings.*
>
> **5** By testing products on these animals, we can learn how they would affect a human being.
>
> → *Testing products on these animals teaches scientists how they might affect a person.*

As you can see, the summary clearly explains the main idea of the reading passage and its supporting details. The paraphrased sentences convey the ideas of the original sentences from the summary with different words.

⊘ Sample Summarizing and Paraphrasing Exercises

You will now listen to the lecture once again. As you listen, complete the summarizing and paraphrasing exercises below. Try to make your answers similar to the ones given for the reading passage.

Summarizing Exercise

alternative methods	not that helpful	very sick
human cells	should be stopped	useful results

Main Idea The lecturer gives two reasons why animal testing _____.

First Supporting Argument For his first argument, the lecturer explains that animal testing
is _____ . He says that animal testing usually does not
produce _____ . The lecturer talks about one medicine that
did not harm mice but made humans _____ .

Second Supporting Argument The lecturer goes on to say that scientists have
_____ to test products. One is using computer models for testing.
Another is using _____ .

Paraphrasing Exercise

1 The lecturer gives two reasons why animal testing should be stopped.

   → *The lecturer gives two reasons why animal testing must not* _____ .

2 For his first argument, the lecturer explains that animal testing is not that helpful.

   → *The lecturer's first argument is that animal testing is not very* _____ .

3 He says that animal testing usually does not produce useful results.

   → *He explains that animal testing often does not* _____ *valuable*
   results.

4 The lecturer talks about one medicine that did not harm mice but made humans very sick.

   → *The lecturer discusses one medicine that did not hurt mice but caused humans to become*
   very _____ .

5 The lecturer goes on to say that scientists have alternative methods to test products.

   → *The lecturer then explains that scientists have* _____ *to test*
   products.

Tandem Note-Taking

Now it is time for you to complete the chart below by using the information from the summarizing and paraphrasing exercises for the reading and the listening. These notes will help you when you write your response.

READING

Main Idea

Animal testing is necessary for important advancements to occur.

First Supporting Argument

Animal testing makes human lives

Supporting Detail

useful in making

Second Supporting Argument

Animal testing is an effective way

Supporting Detail

some animals very similar

LISTENING

Main Idea

The professor argues that animal testing must not continue.

First Supporting Argument

Animal testing is not very

Supporting Detail

medicine did not make mice sick but

Second Supporting Argument

Scientists have other ways

Supporting Detail

using human cells;

Writing Exercise

Use this page to write your response. You have 20 minutes to complete your essay.

Writing Guide	Summarize the points made in the lecture, being sure to explain how they challenge specific claims made in the reading passage.

First Paragraph ○

State and discuss thesis

_____

_____

_____

_____

_____

Second Paragraph ○

First main idea from lecture

Contradiction from reading

Supporting detail

_____

_____

_____

_____

_____

Third Paragraph ○

Second main idea from lecture

Contradiction from reading

Supporting detail

_____

_____

_____

_____

_____

Fourth Paragraph ○

Conclusion (optional)

_____

_____

_____

_____

_____

Sample Response

Read the response carefully to see what makes a response strong. Place the following titles in the appropriate blanks in the response.

> a. Contradictory sentence (×2)   b. Topic sentence (×2)   c. Thesis statement
>
> d. Opening sentence   e. Example (×2)

[   ] The reading passage argues that animal testing is necessary for important advancements to occur. [   ] On the other hand, the professor feels that animal testing must not continue.

[   ] The lecturer's first argument is that animal testing is not that useful. He claims that animal tests usually do not produce helpful results. [   ] To explain this, the professor talks about one medicine tested on mice. The medicine did not make the mice sick. However, it made people very sick. [   ] This contrasts the idea given in the reading passage. It argues that animal testing makes human lives better. It states that it is useful in making medicine.

[   ] For his second argument, the speaker states that scientists have other ways to test products. [   ] One of these ways is using human cells. This is beneficial because it does not hurt living creatures. It is also more accurate than testing animals. Another method is using computer modeling. [   ] The passage makes a different argument. It states that animal testing is the best way to test products. The reason is that some animals are very similar to human beings.

Integrated Writing Scoring Rubric

The scoring rubric below is similar to the one used by the TOEFL® iBT Writing Task graders.

Score 5

A response scoring a 5 clearly summarizes the central ideas from the lecture. It also explains how they relate to the arguments given in the reading passage. Essays of this level are well organized and contain very few grammatical errors that do not make the meaning unclear.

Score 4

A response scoring at this level usually does a good job of presenting the main ideas from the lecture and explaining how they relate to those presented in the reading passage. However, it may occasionally be unclear or inaccurate. A response will also earn a score of 4 if it includes more grammatical errors that only occasionally make the meaning unclear.

Score 3

A response scoring at this level generally explains the main ideas from the lecture and how they relate to those presented in the reading passage. However, the explanations may be vague, unclear, or sometimes incorrect. A response that does not include one of the main ideas from the lecture will also score at this level. Finally, essays of this level may contain more frequent grammatical errors that make it difficult to understand the relationship between the arguments made in the lecture and the reading passage.

Score 2

A response scoring at this level includes only some of the important ideas from the lecture and fails to explain how they relate to the information presented in the reading passage. A response scoring a 2 may also include serious grammatical errors that prevent readers who are not already familiar with the topic from understanding the main ideas from the lecture and the reading passage.

Score 1

A response scoring at this level includes little or no useful information from the lecture or the reading passage. It may also include very low-level language that completely obscures the meaning of the response.

Score 0

A response scoring at this level simply copies sentences from the reading, does not address the topic, is written in a foreign language, or has no writing.

Explanation of the Independent Writing Task

The Independent Writing Task is the second half of the TOEFL® iBT writing section. Students have 30 minutes to write an essay explaining their options about a given question. Responses should be between 300 and 400 words long. To earn a top score, test takers must use clear arguments and examples to support their arguments. Strong responses are usually four or five paragraphs long. The introductory paragraph comes first. Next come two or three supporting paragraphs with clear topic sentences. The last part is the concluding paragraph.

Independent Writing Task Wording

There are three possible writing tasks you will be presented with. However, they all ask you to express your opinion about an important issue.

For the agree/disagree type, the task will be presented in the following way:

▶ Do you agree or disagree with the following statement?

[A sentence or sentences that present an issue]

Use specific reasons and examples to support your answer.

cf. *This question type accounts for almost all of the essay topics that have been asked on the TOEFL® iBT so far.*

For the preference type, the task will be presented in the following way:

▶ Some people say X. Others believe Y. Which opinion do you agree with? Use specific reasons and examples to support your answer.

▶ Some people do X. Other people do Y. Which . . . do you think is better? Use specific reasons and examples to support your opinion.

For the opinion type, the task will be presented in the following way:

▶ In your opinion, what is the most important . . . ? Use specific reasons and examples from your experience to explain your answer.

▶ **[A sentence or sentences that state a fact]**

In your opinion, what is one thing that should be . . . ? Use specific reasons and details to explain your choice.

Writing Tips for the Independent Writing Task

- Spend three to five minutes brainstorming and organizing your response before you begin writing.

- Rewrite the question in your thesis statement.

- Include two or three main ideas in your essay to support your opinion.

- Give supporting ideas and examples from your personal experience and knowledge to improve your response.

- Manage your time wisely. Try not to spend more than five to seven minutes writing each paragraph.

- Use the last one to three minutes to proofread your response. Correct errors as needed.

Sample Independent Writing Task

On the Independent Writing Task, you will be given the following directions along with a similar writing prompt:

Directions Read the question below. You have 30 minutes to plan, write, and revise your essay. Typically, an effective response will contain a minimum of 300 words.

Question

Do you agree or disagree with the following statement?

Getting advice from people who are older than you is more valuable than getting advice from your peers.

Use specific reasons and examples to support your answer.

Understanding the Background

Generating ideas is one of the most difficult parts of the Independent Writing Task. Read the following background information to learn more about the topic given above.

Getting advice from people who are older than you is often a good idea. For one, older people have probably faced problems similar to yours when they were younger. In addition, older people are better at understanding the effects of a decision. They know how a bad decision can affect your life later on. Finally, people who are older have more knowledge. They may know of better solutions to problems that younger people might not know.

On the other hand, there are times when getting advice from your peers is better. First, people your own age may understand your situation better. They might be experiencing the same problems as you. Asking younger people for advice may be more comfortable. For instance, asking someone much older about dating advice might be awkward. Lastly, your peers can understand how decisions can affect your friendships. For social matters, asking younger people is usually better.

⊘ **Sample Understanding the Background Exercise**

Use the background information to complete the sentences below.

1 People your age might be experiencing the _____ as you.

2 Older people better understand the _____ of a decision.

3 People who are older may have faced _____ when they were younger.

4 Getting _____ from an older person might be awkward.

5 Someone who is older has _____ than a younger person.

6 Older people are more likely to understand how a bad decision can affect your life _____ .

7 Your peers are more likely to _____ better.

8 Asking younger people is usually better for _____ .

Selecting and Generating Ideas

⊘ Sample Selecting Ideas Exercise

Read the phrases below. Decide whether they agree or disagree with the given statement. Then, write the sentences on the correct lines below and circle the topic sentences.

- People your age will probably understand your situation better.
- There are some situations when it is better to ask your peers for advice.
- People who are older can better understand the long-term effects of a decision.

- Older people generally have more life experience.
- It is often better to get advice from older people.
- Asking peers for social advice is usually more valuable.

Agree

_____

_____

_____

Disagree

_____

_____

_____

⊘ Sample Generating Ideas Exercise

Use the ideas you chose in the Selecting Ideas exercise to fill in the blanks below.

Agree
1. Getting advice from older people is _____ .
2. People who are older have more _____ than younger people.
3. Older people can understand how a decision can affect your life in the _____ .

Disagree
1. In some situations, getting advice _____ is more valuable.
2. Your peers are more likely to understand _____ .
3. Asking people your age for advice can be _____ .

Outlining Exercise

To be successful on the writing portion of the TOEFL®, you must outline your essay before you begin writing. Begin by writing your thesis statement. Then, logically arrange your supporting ideas. Finally, write down at least one supporting example for each supporting idea.

⊘ Planning

Use the outline to plan your response to the following: **Do you agree or disagree with the following statement? Getting advice from people who are older than you is more valuable than getting advice from your peers. Use specific reasons and examples to support your answer.**

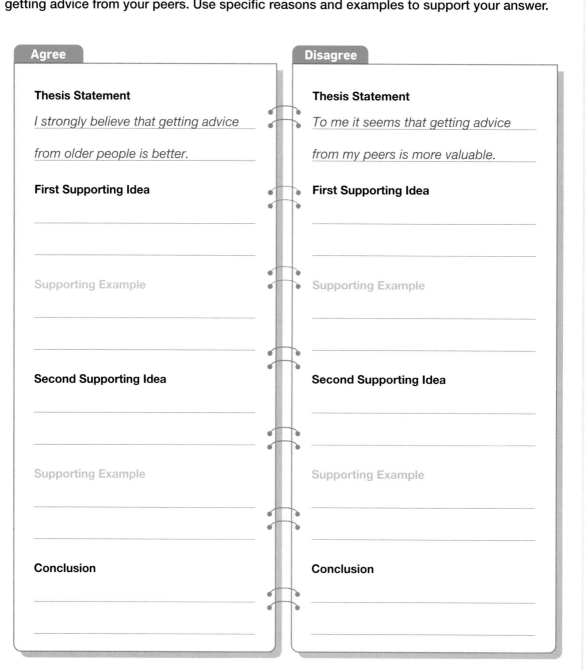

Agree

Thesis Statement

I strongly believe that getting advice from older people is better.

First Supporting Idea

Supporting Example

Second Supporting Idea

Supporting Example

Conclusion

Disagree

Thesis Statement

To me it seems that getting advice from my peers is more valuable.

First Supporting Idea

Supporting Example

Second Supporting Idea

Supporting Example

Conclusion

Writing Exercise

Use this page to write your response. You have 30 minutes to complete your essay.

First Paragraph

State and discuss thesis

_____
_____
_____
_____
_____

Second Paragraph

First main supporting idea

Supporting detail

Example

_____
_____
_____
_____
_____
_____

Third Paragraph

Second main supporting idea

Supporting detail

Example

_____
_____
_____
_____
_____
_____

Fourth Paragraph

Conclusion

_____
_____
_____
_____
_____

Sample Response

Read the response carefully to see what makes a response strong. Place the following titles in the appropriate blanks in the response.

a. Summary   b. Opening sentences   c. General statement (×2)   d. Thesis statement
e. Example (×2)   f. Topic sentence (×2)   g. Final comment

[   ] When faced with a difficult situation, it is important to get advice from other people. Some people may feel that getting advice from someone older is best. [   ] As for me, I think getting advice from people the same age is more valuable.

[   ] To begin with, your peers are more likely to understand your problem. [   ] They might have recently experienced a similar situation. This means that they can give you more appropriate advice. [   ] This is what happened when I tried to get my driver's license. I wanted to know what the driving test was like. So I asked my friends about it. Many of them had recently gotten their driver's licenses. They were therefore able to give me advice about the same situation.

[   ] Furthermore, getting advice from people your own age can be more comfortable. [   ] It is easier to talk about some things with your peers than with people who are older. [   ] In my case, I chose to ask my friends for advice on dating. I asked them what I should do on a date and what I should avoid doing. Of course, older people have gone on dates before. But talking about dating with a teacher or a parent is awkward. For sensitive topics, I feel that getting advice from my peers is better.

[   ] Getting advice is the best way to make intelligent decisions. There may be certain times when getting advice from an older person is better. [   ] However, for the reasons given, I believe getting advice from peers is a better idea in most situations.

Independent Writing Scoring Rubric

The scoring rubric below is similar to the one used by the TOEFL® iBT Writing Task graders.

Score 5

An essay that earns a 5 clearly addresses the topic. It uses logical organization, correct transitions between ideas and paragraphs, and developed supporting examples for each main idea. The essay reads smoothly and includes a variety of sentence types, suitable word choice, and correct use of idiomatic expressions. It may also include minor grammatical errors that do not distract the reader.

Score 4

An essay scoring at this level does a good job of addressing the topic. However, it may not include details that fully develop its supporting ideas. It is clearly organized for the most part though it may include some unclear transitions, redundancies, and/or unrelated information. It may also include more noticeable errors in grammar and word choice that do not obscure the meaning.

Score 3

An essay that earns a 3 addresses the topic by using explanations and examples that are not easily understood or fully developed. Although the response is somewhat coherent, it may not have clear transitions between ideas. An essay scoring at this level may also include accurate but limited sentence structures and vocabulary and more frequent grammatical errors that occasionally obscure the meaning.

Score 2

An essay scoring at this level fails to address the topic clearly and is characterized by inadequate organization and insufficiently developed ideas. It may include examples that fail to develop the main ideas and more numerous grammatical errors that obscure the meaning.

Score 1

An essay scoring at this level fails to present and develop any ideas and includes serious and frequent grammatical errors that largely obscure the meaning.

Score 0

A response scoring at this level simply copies the topic, does not address the topic, is written in a foreign language, or has no writing.

Part B

Building Knowledge & Skills for the Writing Test

Linguistics: **Learning a Foreign Language**

🎯 **Vocabulary** Take a few moments to review the vocabulary items that will appear in this task.

- **globalized** *adj.* going across the entire world
  Today, we live in a **globalized** world.

- **society** *n.* the system of community life
  Korean **society** is much different from American society.

- **conduct** *v.* to lead; to do
  The scientists **conducted** an experiment on monkeys.

- **communicate** *v.* to exchange ideas by writing or speaking
  I like to **communicate** with my friends over the Internet.

- **international** *adj.* involving two or more nations
  I work at an **international** company that has offices in the United States and China.

- **especially** *adv.* mainly; in particular
  The weather here is **especially** hot during summer.

- **widely** *adv.* across a large distance
  Ian has traveled **widely**. He has been to Africa, Asia, and South America.

- **value** *v.* to understand the importance of; to appreciate
  I **value** our friendship very much.

- **essential** *adj.* needed; necessary
  Water is **essential** for life.

- **successful** *adj.* wealthy; popular
  Bill Gates is a highly **successful** businessman.

Words and Expressions Refer to the vocabulary to fill in the blanks below. You may need to change the forms of the words.

1 Tom Cruise is one of the most _____ known actors in the world.

2 I love her new style, _____ the gold earrings.

3 _____ shapes the way people think and act.

4 _____ people work hard every day.

5 The world has become _____ thanks to the Internet and airplane travel.

6 I usually use my cell phone to _____ with other people.

7 Exercising and eating a healthy diet are _____ for losing weight.

8 The government will _____ research on the lives of poor people.

9 Of all the things in the world, I _____ my health the most.

10 Taking _____ flights is much more expensive than flying in one's home country.

Reading

Read the passage carefully. Try to understand what the main argument of the passage is. You have 3 minutes to read.

Today, we live in a globalized society. People from all over the world conduct business with one another all the time. They often meet other people who do not speak the same language. So these people need a way to communicate with each other. For this reason, everybody must study a foreign language at school.

Many companies today do international business. These companies need employees with foreign language skills. This is especially true when a country's language is not widely spoken. A good example of this is Swedish. However, even employees who speak international languages such as English and French should learn a second language. This will allow them to communicate with a greater number of people. Overall, people with foreign language skills help improve the economy. This is why young people must learn second languages.

Studying a foreign language also helps students get good jobs. Employers value people who can speak more than one language. They know that foreign languages are essential for business. As a result, people who speak a second language can get jobs more easily. Workers with foreign language skills usually earn more money as well. By learning a foreign language as students, these people can be more successful as adults.

Summarizing Read the information below. Use the information to complete the summary of the reading passage.

foreign languages	essential for business	international business
good jobs	around the world	second language

Main Idea The author of the reading passage believes that students should study _____ . The reason is that being able to communicate with people from _____ is very important in business.

First Supporting Argument The first argument the author gives is that companies need employees who can speak a _____ . The reason is that these companies do _____ .

Second Supporting Argument The author's next reason is that learning a foreign language helps students get _____ . Employers understand that foreign languages are _____ .

◎ Vocabulary
Take a few moments to review the vocabulary items that will appear in this task.

- **survey** *n.* the questioning of people to learn their opinions about a topic

  Stores sometimes ask customers to fill out **surveys**.

- **subject** *n.* a course; an area of study

  My favorite **subject** at school is history.

- **trouble** *n.* something that causes problems

  My son causes a lot of **trouble** at school.

- **concentrate** *v.* to think about; to focus on

  Please be quiet. I'm trying to **concentrate** on this math problem.

- **develop** *v.* to increase little by little; to expand

  Developing good foreign language speaking skills takes many years.

- **native language** *n.* the language a person learns from birth; a first language

  My **native language** is French, but I also speak English and German.

- **require** *v.* to be in need of; to want

  Everyone is **required** to show an ID at the door.

- **bank teller** *n.* a person who works at a bank and gives and receives money

  My friend works as a **bank teller**.

Words and Expressions Refer to the vocabulary to fill in the blanks below. You may need to change the forms of the words.

1 A person's _____ affects that individual's ability to learn foreign languages.

2 Some people can _____ more easily when they listen to music.

3 I want to be a _____ when I grow up.

4 Math is a difficult _____ for many students.

5 This class _____ you to complete three research papers.

6 According to recent _____, the number of people without jobs has increased.

7 Exercising regularly helps _____ the muscles throughout your body.

8 I was late for work this morning because I had car _____.

Listening

Now listen to part of a lecture on the topic you just read about.

02-01

Summarizing
Read the information below. Use the information to complete the summary of the lecture.

concentrate on developing	bank teller	native language
not needed	is against	other subjects

Main Idea The professor explains that students should study _____ rather than study a foreign language.

First Supporting Argument First, she argues that most children cannot read or write their _____ very well. Therefore, they need to _____ these skills first.

Second Supporting Argument The professor also believes that knowing a foreign language is _____ for most jobs. She gives the example of a(n) _____. Overall, the professor _____ the idea of learning a foreign language.

Paraphrasing Exercise

Reading   The following sentences come from the reading passage summary. Complete each paraphrase with the appropriate words or phrases.

1   The author of the reading passage believes that students should study foreign languages.

→ *The writer of the reading passage _____ that students should study foreign languages.*

2   The first argument the author gives is that companies need employees who can speak a foreign language.

→ *The author's first supporting argument is that companies need _____ who know a foreign language.*

3   The reason is that these companies do international business.

→ *The reason is that these companies do business in _____ countries.*

4   The author's next reason is that learning a foreign language helps students get good jobs.

→ *Next, the author argues that studying a _____ language helps students find good jobs.*

5   Employers understand that foreign languages are essential for business.

→ *Employers realize that foreign languages are _____ for business.*

Listening   The following sentences come from the lecture summary. Complete each paraphrase with the appropriate words or phrases.

1   The professor explains that students should study other subjects rather than study a foreign language.

→ *The instructor argues that students should _____ other subjects rather than study a second language.*

2   First, she argues that most children cannot read or write their native language very well.

→ *Her first argument is that most students cannot _____ their native language very well.*

3   Therefore, they need to concentrate on developing these skills first.

→ *For this reason, students need to _____ on developing their native language abilities first.*

4   The professor also believes that knowing a foreign language is not needed for most jobs.

→ *Next, the professor states that _____ a foreign language is not needed for most jobs.*

5   Overall, the professor is against the idea of learning a foreign language.

→ *On the whole, the professor does not _____ the idea of studying a second language.*

Tandem Note-Taking

Refer to the summary exercises for the reading and the listening. Paraphrase them to complete the side-by-side notes below. Include only the two points from the reading and the listening that clearly contradict each other.

Main Idea

Students need to learn a foreign language

to be successful in today's world.

First Supporting Argument

Businesses need employees who can

speak a

Supporting Detail

especially true when a country's language

is not

Second Supporting Argument

Knowing a foreign language helps

students

Supporting Detail

can get good jobs more   ;

can also earn more

Main Idea

Students should focus on other subjects

rather than learn a second language.

First Supporting Argument

Most students are not able to use their

Supporting Detail

cannot get a good job or

Second Supporting Argument

Most jobs do not require foreign

language

Supporting Detail

bank tellers do not need a foreign   ;

customers speak

Writing

Use this page to write your response. You have 20 minutes to complete your essay.

Writing Guide

Summarize the points made in the lecture, being sure to explain how they challenge specific claims made in the reading passage.

First Paragraph ◌

State and discuss thesis

Second Paragraph ◌

First main idea from reading

Contradiction from lecture

Supporting detail

Third Paragraph ◌

Second main idea from reading

Contradiction from lecture

Supporting detail

Fourth Paragraph ◌

Conclusion (optional)

✕**SCAFFOLDING** Here are some useful phrases to help you when you write.

✓ The topic of the reading and the lecture is…

✓ The reading passage argues in favor of…

✓ The professor, on the other hand…

✓ First, the author of the reading passage believes that…

✓ In the lecture, the professor argues…

✓ Next, the reading passages states that…

✓ Again, the professor…

✓ She contends that most students…

Sample Response

Read the response carefully to see what makes a response strong.

The topic of the reading and the lecture is learning foreign languages. The reading passage argues in favor of learning foreign languages. The professor, on the other hand, is against learning foreign languages.

First, the author of the reading passage believes that companies need workers who speak foreign languages. They need people who speak many languages because they do business in many countries. In the lecture, the professor argues that most students do not need to learn a foreign language. She believes this because many young students cannot use their native language well. Therefore, they should develop these skills first.

Next, the reading passage states that speaking a foreign language helps students get jobs easily. Employers want people who speak more than one language because it is essential for business. **1** Again, the professor disagrees. **2** She feels that many jobs do not require foreign language skills. **3**

Critical Analysis Refer to the sample response to complete the tasks below.

1 Which of the following sentences is the thesis statement of the response?

- Ⓐ Next, the reading passage states that speaking a foreign language helps students get jobs easily.
- Ⓑ The professor, on the other hand, is against learning foreign languages.
- Ⓒ First, the author of the reading passage believes that companies need workers who speak foreign languages.

2 Where should the following sentence be added to improve the response?

To explain this, the professor mentions bank tellers.

- Ⓐ **1**
- Ⓑ **2**
- Ⓒ **3**

3 Which word in the response means "**to expand**"?

4 List the connecting phrase the writer of the response uses in the first paragraph.

Teaching Responsibility with Pets

? Question

Do you agree or disagree with the following statement? The best way to teach children about responsibility is by having them care for an animal. Use specific reasons and examples to support your answer.

Background & Brainstorming

Read the following background information to learn more about the topic.

Pro

Children can learn a lot about responsibility by caring for a pet. First, they understand that pets are living creatures. They find out that pets need food and water regularly just like people. Second, they learn that pets can get hurt and need to go to the hospital. Finally, pets teach children that animals have feelings, too. By caring for a pet, children can learn how to be responsible adults and good parents.

Con

There are many drawbacks to children having a pet. For one, young children may not know how to treat a pet properly. This can seriously hurt the pet. Sometimes the pet may even hurt the child. Furthermore, most children do not have much patience. So they end up not caring for the pet after a short time. This means that parents have to take care of the animal. Therefore, children may not really learn about responsibility with a pet after all.

Understanding the Background Use the background information to complete the sentences below.

1   Children can learn about responsibility by _____ for a pet.

2   Sometimes young children may not understand how to _____ their pets properly.

3   Children learn that animals have _____ from their pets.

4   Pets can _____ and need to go the hospital just like people do.

5   Many children do not have a lot of _____, so they do not care for their pets.

6   Caring for a pet can teach children how to be _____ and good parents.

7   _____ may have to care for the pets instead of their children.

8   Children learn that animals need _____ regularly.

Selecting Ideas Read the sentences below. Decide whether they agree or disagree with the given statement. Then, write the sentences on the correct lines below and circle the topic sentences.

- Pets will not survive without receiving food and water from their owners.

- Children should learn about responsibility in other ways.

- Children learn about taking care of another living creature.

- Many parents of young children usually end up caring for the pet.

- Caring for a pet is a great way to teach children about responsibility.

- Many children are too young to handle pets properly.

Agree

Disagree

Generating Ideas Use the ideas you chose in the Selecting Ideas exercise to fill in the blanks below.

Agree

1 Children must give their pets _____ regularly in order for them to survive.

2 Pets teach children how to care for another _____ .

3 Caring for a pet is an excellent way to teach children about _____ .

Disagree

1 There are _____ to teach children about responsibility.

2 Children that are too young cannot _____ pets properly.

3 Parents with young children usually end up _____ for the pet instead.

Developing Ideas You have now examined the two options. Which of the two do you feel more comfortable developing into an essay? Explain why you feel this way.

▌Planning

Do you agree or disagree with the following statement? The best way to teach children about responsibility is by having them care for an animal. Use specific reasons and examples to support your answer.

Agree

Thesis Statement

I feel that the best way to teach children

about responsibility is by caring for an animal.

First Supporting Idea

_____

_____

_____

Supporting Example

_____

_____

Second Supporting Idea

_____

_____

_____

Supporting Example

_____

_____

Conclusion

_____

_____

Disagree

Thesis Statement

I believe there are better ways to teach

responsibility than caring for an animal.

First Supporting Idea

_____

_____

_____

Supporting Example

_____

_____

Second Supporting Idea

_____

_____

_____

Supporting Example

_____

_____

Conclusion

_____

_____

Writing

Use this page to write your response. You have 30 minutes to complete your essay.

First Paragraph ▷

State and discuss thesis

_____
_____
_____

Second Paragraph ▷

First main supporting idea

Supporting detail

Example

_____
_____
_____
_____
_____

Third Paragraph ▷

Second main supporting idea

Supporting detail

Example

_____
_____
_____
_____
_____

Fourth Paragraph ▷

Conclusion

_____
_____
_____
_____

✂ **SCAFFOLDING**   Here are some useful phrases to help you when you write.

✓ I agree that caring for animals is…

✓ I feel this way for two…

✓ One reason that pets are (not) a good way to teach children about…

✓ To explain, I will give a personal…

✓ Second, children develop a bond with…

✓ For instance, when I was younger, I had…

✓ Children can definitely learn a lot from…

✓ For the reasons given above, it is obvious that…

Read the response carefully to see what makes a response strong.

I agree that caring for animals is the best way to teach children about responsibility. I believe this because many children enjoy taking care of pets. In addition, children with pets develop emotional bonds with their animals.

One reason that pets are a good way to teach responsibility is that children enjoy taking care of pets. Children feel good when their pet is happy. To explain, I will give a personal example. When I was young, my first pet was a hamster. I made sure to take good care of her every day. I fed her regularly and cleaned her cage every day. This made my hamster very happy. She would run excitedly around her cage. Because I took good care of her, she lived a long time. This experience taught me that you should be responsible if you have a pet.

Second, children develop bonds with their animals. They begin to love their pets and feel like they have to care for them. This bond helps children become more responsible. For instance, my sister got a dog when she was a teenager. She learned to take very good care of her dog. She fed the dog regularly and took him for walks after school every day. As a result, she still has her dog today. Clearly, children can learn a lot about responsibility from pets.

There are many ways children can learn about responsibility. But for the reasons given above, it is obvious that children can learn a lot by taking care of pets.

Critical Analysis Refer to the sample response to complete the tasks below.

1 Which of the following sentences is the topic sentence in the second paragraph?

　Ⓐ Because I took good care of her, she lived a long time.

　Ⓑ One reason that pets are a good way to teach responsibility is that children enjoy taking care of pets.

　Ⓒ This experience taught me that you should be responsible if you have a pet.

2 Which sentence below is closest in meaning to the underlined sentence?

　Ⓐ Pets only love and care for owners that take good care of them.

　Ⓑ Owners that take good care of their pets usually love them more.

　Ⓒ Children start to feel deeply about their pets and want to treat them well.

3 List the connecting word the writer uses in the last paragraph.

Part B

Zoology: **The Eyes of the Giant Squid**

🎯 Vocabulary Take a few moments to review the vocabulary items that will appear in this task.

- **impressive** *adj.* able to create a positive opinion
  She gave an **impressive** speech to the audience.

- **roughly** *adv.* around; about
  It will take **roughly** thirty minutes to bake the cake.

- **hypothesize** *v.* to believe; to come up with a theory
  The scientist **hypothesizes** about the reason the animals behave that way.

- **dive** *v.* to go down deep in the water
  The submarine can **dive** to the bottom of the sea.

- **gather** *v.* to collect
  They will **gather** berries from the bushes in the field.

- **predator** *n.* an animal that hunts other animals to kill and eat
  All the animals are running away from the **predator**.

- **detect** *v.* to see; to find, often after looking for something
  They are trying to **detect** any problems with the machine.

- **flee** *v.* to run away; to try to escape from
  The animals started to **flee** from the hungry lion.

- **survive** *v.* to stay alive
  Everyone on the ship **survived** when it sank.

- **encounter** *n.* a meeting
  The swimmer had a close **encounter** with a shark.

Words and Expressions Refer to the vocabulary to fill in the blanks below. You may need to change the forms of the words.

1 Many small animals _____ when there is danger.

2 What do you _____ is the reason this happened?

3 The human eye _____ light and helps people see.

4 We cannot _____ any problems at all.

5 He spent an _____ amount of money at the shopping center.

6 She had an unpleasant _____ with an unhappy customer.

7 Some whales can _____ thousands of meters under the water.

8 It can be hard to _____ when a tornado hits.

9 There are _____ 1,000 people in the stadium.

10 Wolves and foxes are both _____ that live in forests.

▌ Reading

Read the passage carefully. Try to understand what the main argument of the passage is. You have 3 minutes to read.

Giant squid are some of nature's most impressive animals. They can grow to be nearly twenty meters long. They also have a huge eye on either side of their head.

Each eye is roughly the size of a dinnerplate. These eyes are much larger than those of other animals. Zoologists think they may know why the eyes are so big. Some hypothesize that the big eyes are useful when hunting. Giant squid can dive 2,000 meters beneath the ocean's surface. The deeper it gets, the darker the ocean becomes. The huge eyes are therefore necessary to gather light. This lets squid see better, so they can hunt well.

There is a second theory about the eyes. While giant squid are predators, they are also hunted by sperm whales. The squid need strong eyes to watch out for sperm whales. Zoologists believe the giant squid can see up to 120 meters. Their strong eyesight lets them detect any sperm whales hunting it. So they can either flee or prepare to fight. The squid's eyes therefore give them a chance to survive an encounter with a deadly sperm whale.

Summarizing Read the information below. Use the information to complete the summary for the reading passage.

flee or fight	gather light	strong eyesight
dive deep	a huge eye	sperm whales

Main Idea The reading passage states that giant squid have _____ on each side of their head.

First Supporting Argument First, the passage claims that the squid's eyes are useful when they hunt. The giant squid can _____ beneath the surface, where it is very dark. The eyes _____ and let the squid see so that they can hunt.

Second Supporting Argument The passage goes on to mention that _____ hunt giant squid. So squid need _____ to help them detect sperm whales. It states that squid can _____ whenever they see a sperm whale.

🎯 Vocabulary Take a few moments to review the vocabulary items that will appear in this task.

enormous *adj.* huge; very large
An elephant is an **enormous** land animal.

pitch black *adj.* very dark
The room was **pitch black**, so we could not see anything.

rely *v.* to depend on
We **rely** on computers very much in the modern age.

tentacle *n.* a long, slender appendage of an animal that is often used to taste or feel
An octopus can use its **tentacles** to help it move.

prey *n.* an animal that is hunted by others for food
Rabbits are often **prey** for hawks and eagles.

capture *v.* to catch
The hunter is using traps to **capture** animals.

locate *v.* to find; to detect
He cannot **locate** his missing bag anywhere.

echolocation *n.* a system like sonar that animals use to detect and locate objects
Bats and dolphins use **echolocation** to find prey.

range *n.* an extent
Wolves hunt on a wide **range** of land.

aware *adj.* knowing about
I am **aware** that there are some problems with the project.

Words and Expressions Refer to the vocabulary to fill in the blanks below. You may need to change the forms of the words.

1 They are trying to _____ the buried treasure.

2 A squid has ten long _____ attached to its body.

3 When a place is _____, it is impossible to see anything.

4 _____ lets bats fly in very dark conditions.

5 It can be hard to _____ some tiny animals.

6 The dinosaurs were _____ creatures when they were alive.

7 This machine has a _____ of capabilities.

8 We were not _____ that any customers were unhappy.

9 _____ animals often flee when there is danger.

10 Try to _____ on yourself instead of depending on others.

Listening

Now listen to part of a lecture on the topic you just read about.

02-02

Summarizing
Read the information below. Use the information to complete the summary for the lecture.

use echolocation	their tentacles	are aware of
with no light	the purposes	from far away

Main Idea In the lecture, the instructor believes that the theories on _____ of the eyes of giant squid have problems. He gives two reasons to support his argument.

First Supporting Argument The instructor's first argument is that giant squid hunt in places _____. Therefore, their eyes cannot help them see well enough to hunt. Instead, the instructor remarks that squid use _____ when they hunt.

Second Supporting Argument Next, the instructor states that sperm whales _____. As a result, they can detect giant squid _____. This means that they _____ giant squid long before the squid know the whales are around.

Paraphrasing Exercise

Reading The following sentences come from the reading passage summary. Complete each paraphrase with the appropriate words or phrases.

1 The reading passage states that giant squid have a huge eye on each side of their head.

   → *The reading passage states that giant squid have a huge eye on* _____
   sides of their head.

2 First, the passage claims that the squid's eyes are useful when they hunt.

   → *First, the passage mentions that the squid's eyes are useful when they are searching for* _____
   _____ *.*

3 The eyes gather light and let the squid see so that they can hunt.

   → *The eyes* _____ *light, so the squid can see well enough to hunt.*

4 The passage goes on to mention that sperm whales hunt giant squid.

   → *The passage next mentions that sperm whales try to* _____ *and eat giant squid.*

5 It states that squid can flee or fight whenever they see a sperm whale.

   → *It states that squid can* _____ *or fight if they encounter a sperm whale.*

Listening The following sentences come from the lecture summary. Complete each paraphrase with the appropriate words or phrases.

1 In the lecture, the instructor believes that the theories on the purposes of the eyes of giant squid have problems.

   → *In the lecture, the instructor comments that each theory on the purpose of giant squid eyes is* _____ *.*

2 The instructor's first argument is that giant squid hunt in places with no light.

   → *The instructor's first argument is that giant squid hunt in* _____ *places.*

3 Instead, the instructor remarks that squid use their tentacles when they hunt.

   → *Rather, the instructor remarks that squid use their tentacles when searching for* _____ *.*

4 Next, the instructor states that sperm whales use echolocation.

   → *Next, the instructor* _____ *that sperm whales use echolocation.*

5 As a result, they can detect giant squid from far away.

   → *As a result, they can find giant squid from great* _____ *.*

Tandem Note-Taking

Refer to the summary exercises for the reading and the listening. Paraphrase them to complete the side-by-side notes below. Include only the two points from the reading and the listening that clearly contradict each other.

Main Idea

The huge eyes of the giant squid have a

couple of purposes.

First Supporting Argument

The eyes help squid see well enough to

Supporting Detail

dive deep; very dark; eyes gather   ;

can see

Second Supporting Argument

The eyes let squid detect

Supporting Detail

strong eyesight helps them find sperm

whales; can

Main Idea

The theories on the purposes of the eyes

of giant squid have problems.

First Supporting Argument

Giant squid hunt in

Supporting Detail

eyes cannot help them see; use

Second Supporting Argument

Sperm whales can detect giant squid by

using

Supporting Detail

can find squid from far away; know about

squid before

Writing

Use this page to write your response. You have 20 minutes to complete your essay.

Writing Guide	Summarize the points made in the lecture, being sure to explain how they cast doubt on specific points made in the reading passage.

First Paragraph ○

State and discuss thesis

_____

_____

_____

Second Paragraph ○

First main idea from lecture

Contradiction from reading

Supporting detail

_____

_____

_____

_____

_____

Third Paragraph ○

Second main idea from lecture

Contradiction from reading

Supporting detail

_____

_____

_____

_____

_____

Fourth Paragraph ○

Conclusion (optional)

_____

_____

_____

_____

✂ **SCAFFOLDING**   Here are some useful phrases to help you when you write.

✓ In the lecture, the instructor…

✓ He argues against the claims in…

✓ The instructor's first argument is…

✓ He points out that…

✓ Second, the instructor disregards…

✓ The instructor notes that…

✓ They can therefore…

✓ This refutes the argument…

Sample Response

Read the response carefully to see what makes a response strong.

In the lecture, the instructor states that the purpose of the giant squid's huge eyes is unknown. He argues against the claims in the reading passage. It argues that zoologists know why the squid has such large eyes.

The instructor's first argument is that giant squid do not need to see well to hunt. He points out that they hunt thousands of meters beneath the surface. There is no light that deep underwater. So squid do not use their eyes when they hunt. Instead, they grab prey with their tentacles whenever they touch something. The instructor argues against the reading passage. It states that giant squid have huge eyes to collect light, which lets them see well enough to hunt.

Second, the instructor disregards the theory that squid need good eyesight to find sperm whales. The instructor notes that sperm whales use echolocation to detect squid. They can therefore find squid from farther away than squid can see. This refutes the argument in the reading passage. It mentions that the strong eyes of giant squid prepare it to flee or to fight sperm whales when it detects them.

Critical Analysis Refer to the sample response to complete the tasks below.

1   Which of the following sentences is the topic sentence of the third paragraph?
   Ⓐ The instructor notes that sperm whales use echolocation to detect squid.
   Ⓑ Second, the instructor disregards the theory that squid need good eyesight to find sperm whales.
   Ⓒ It mentions that the strong eyes of giant squid prepare it to flee or to fight sperm whales when it detects them.

2   Which of the following sentences would best fit in the blank space in the response?
   Ⓐ In fact, the water is pitch black that far down.
   Ⓑ The giant squid does not stay down deep for too long.
   Ⓒ Not many animals live deep beneath the surface.

3   Which word in the response means "**ignores**"?

4   List the two connecting phrases the writer of the response uses in the second paragraph.

Young People Need More Exercise

? Question

Do you agree or disagree with the following statement? Young people today need to get more exercise. Use specific reasons and examples to support your answer.

▌ Background & Brainstorming

Read the following background information to learn more about the topic.

Are Today's Children Exercising Enough?

By Audrey Meyers
November 28, 2010

According to a recent study, today's young people do not get enough exercise. In past years, children used to walk to school and play outside. Now, children's parents drive them to school. Children also spend a lot of time sitting around watching TV and using the computer. Furthermore, doctors warn that children eat too many foods that are high in fat and calories. These include snacks and fast foods. They worry that children do not know the value of staying healthy. Therefore, they believe that children need to get more exercise.

But not everyone believes that children need to worry about losing weight. It is true that many children are active and healthy. Only a small percentage of young people are overweight. The principal at a local elementary school argues that all students at her school take physical education classes. These classes help children stay in shape. Some nutritionists also warn that diet programs can be too difficult for children to do alone. They feel that forcing children to exercise can cause them a lot of stress.

Understanding the Background Use the background information to complete the sentences below.

1 In past years, children _____ to school and played outside.

2 Doctors worry that children do not know the _____ of staying healthy.

3 Schools have _____ classes to make sure that children get exercise.

4 Not everyone believes that children need to worry about _____ .

5 Many foods young people eat today are high in _____ .

6 Today's young people do not get enough _____ .

7 Many children are _____ while only a few are overweight.

8 Some believe that _____ are too difficult for children to do by themselves.

Read the sentences below. Decide whether they agree or disagree with the given statement. Then, write the sentences on the correct lines below and circle the topic sentences.

- Most children stay busy and are in good health.

- Young people today need to get more exercise.

- Exercise programs can be dangerous for children.

- Children are too young to worry about losing weight.

- Today's young people have unhealthy lifestyles.

- Children eat foods that are not good for them.

Agree

_____

_____

_____

Disagree

_____

_____

_____

Generating Ideas Use the ideas you chose in the Selecting Ideas exercise to fill in the blanks below.

Agree

1 Today's young people do not _____ often enough.

2 Young people eat foods that are _____ .

3 Children these days do not live _____ .

Disagree

1 Young people are no _____ to think about weight loss.

2 Children can _____ themselves if they exercise.

3 Young people are usually _____ and already healthy.

Developing Ideas You have now examined the two options. Which of the two do you feel more comfortable developing into an essay? Explain why you feel this way.

Planning

Do you agree or disagree with the following statement? Young people today need to get more exercise. Use specific reasons and examples to support your answer.

Agree	Disagree
Thesis Statement	**Thesis Statement**
It is my opinion that young children do not get enough exercise these days.	*I contend that children are not old enough to worry about losing weight.*
First Supporting Idea	**First Supporting Idea**
Supporting Example	Supporting Example
Second Supporting Idea	**Second Supporting Idea**
Supporting Example	Supporting Example
Conclusion	**Conclusion**

Writing

Use this page to write your response. You have 30 minutes to complete your essay.

| Writing Guide | Do you agree or disagree with the following statement? Young people today need to get more exercise. Use specific reasons and examples to support your answer. |

First Paragraph

State and discuss thesis

_____

_____

_____

Second Paragraph

First main supporting idea

Supporting detail

Example

_____

_____

_____

_____

_____

Third Paragraph

Second main supporting idea

Supporting detail

Example

_____

_____

_____

_____

_____

Fourth Paragraph

Conclusion

_____

_____

_____

_____

SCAFFOLDING Here are some useful phrases to help you when you write.

✓ Some people worry that young people…

✓ First of all, most young children…

✓ Furthermore, children naturally enjoy…

✓ These include activities such as…

✓ Moreover, exercise programs can be…

✓ However, most children are too young to…

✓ Children can hurt themselves if…

✓ Overall, I believe that children…

Read the response carefully to see what makes a response strong.

Some people worry that young people today do not get enough exercise. However, I am not one of those people. I contend that children do not need to worry about losing weight.

First of all, most young children stay busy and are in good health. Children have physical education classes at school. These classes give young people plenty of time to exercise. They also teach children about keeping fit. Furthermore, children naturally enjoy physical activities. These include activities such as riding bicycles and playing tag. In actuality, only a small percentage of children are dangerously overweight. Most young people are already in good health.

Moreover, exercise programs can be dangerous. Exercising to lose weight should be done in a specific manner. It should not be done without the help of a doctor. However, most children are too young to follow such programs. Children can hurt themselves if they try to start an exercise program. This can be more dangerous than being overweight. Because of this, children should not exercise to lose weight. Overweight children can start an exercise program when they are old enough to do it properly.

Overall, I believe that children are too young to worry about weight loss. Most children are already in good health. And exercise programs can be dangerous for young people.

Critical Analysis Refer to the sample response to complete the tasks below.

1   Which of the following sentences is the thesis statement of the response?

    Ⓐ Some people worry that young people today do not get enough exercise.

    Ⓑ I contend that children do not need to worry about losing weight.

    Ⓒ To begin with, most young children stay busy and are in good health.

2   Which sentence below is closest in meaning to the underlined sentence?

    Ⓐ Exercising can be more harmful for children than being overweight.

    Ⓑ Overweight children should avoid getting too much exercise if possible.

    Ⓒ Young people should only exercise if they talk to a doctor first.

3   List the three connecting phrases the writer uses in the second paragraph.

Part B

Biology: **Could Tyrannosaurus Rex Run?**

🎯 **Vocabulary** Take a few moments to review the vocabulary items that will appear in this task.

- **perhaps** *adv.* maybe; possibly
  This huge diamond is **perhaps** the most expensive one ever found in the world.

- **hunter** *n.* an animal that kills and eats other animals
  Sharks, lions, and human beings are all **hunters**.

- **remain** *v.* to stay in the same condition
  The only thing that **remains** from the house after the fire is its chimney.

- **injure** *v.* to get hurt; to be harmed
  Professional athletes often **injure** themselves.

- **force** *n.* power; energy
  The **force** of the wave knocked me over.

- **gravity** *n.* the force that pulls objects toward a planet
  The **gravity** on Mars is about the same as it is on Earth.

- **severe** *adj.* causing great damage; extreme
  The destruction from the typhoon was **severe**.

- **mass** *n.* the weight of an object
  Larger objects usually have more **mass** than smaller objects.

Words and Expressions Refer to the vocabulary to fill in the blanks below. You may need to change the forms of the words.

1 The deer were scared off when one of the _____ made a sudden noise.

2 Even a small earthquake has enough _____ to destroy a large building.

3 The _____ of one blue whale is nearly 150 tons.

4 Please _____ seated until the plane comes to a complete stop.

5 Our company currently faces a(n) _____ shortage of qualified staff.

6 _____ we should get going. It is already ten o'clock.

7 When you are in outer space, you become taller because there is no _____ .

8 If you do not follow our safety rules, then you may _____ yourself badly.

Reading

Read the passage carefully. Try to understand what the main argument of the passage is. You have 3 minutes to read.

Tyrannosaurus rex was perhaps the greatest dinosaur hunter. Today, it is one of the best-known dinosaurs. Movies and television programs often show Tyrannosaurus rex as a fast animal. However, in reality, Tyrannosaurus rex was probably not able to run.

First, Tyrannosaurus rex was extremely heavy. An adult weighed between six and eight tons. This means that the animal's bones were probably not strong enough to allow it to run. Moreover, a Tyrannosaurus rex would have been easily injured if it had tried to run. If it fell while running, its body would have hit the ground at six times the force of gravity. This would have caused severe injury or even death.

Second, Tyrannosaurus rex did not have very large leg muscles. In order to run at high speeds, an animal must have large leg muscles. Its muscles must be larger than fifty percent of its total mass. The leg muscles of a Tyrannosaurus rex were probably only twenty-five percent of its mass. This means that Tyrannosaurus rex probably could not run all that fast. Most likely, it could run about twenty kilometers per hour.

Summarizing Read the information below. Use the information to complete the summary of the reading passage.

too heavy	fifty percent	leg muscles
could not run	severe injury	twenty-five percent
bones		

Main Idea The reading passage argues that Tyrannosaurus rex _____ .

First Supporting Argument One supporting idea given is that Tyrannosaurus rex was _____ to run. Its _____ were not strong enough to allow it run. If a Tyrannosaurus rex fell while running, it would have suffered a _____ .

Second Supporting Argument The second supporting idea is that Tyrannosaurus rex did not have large enough _____ to run. Its leg muscles were _____ of its mass. But it would have needed muscles larger than _____ of its mass to run.

◎ Vocabulary Take a few moments to review the vocabulary items that will appear in this task.

- **excellent** *adj.* very good; of the highest quality
  Thank you for doing such an **excellent** job. The house has never looked cleaner.

- **debate** *v.* to argue for or against something
  The children **debated** with their parents about where to go for dinner.

- **hollow** *adj.* having empty space on the inside
  The body of a guitar is **hollow** to make sounds louder.

- **risk** *n.* a possibility of suffering harm; a danger
  To be successful in life, you have to be willing to take **risks**.

- **flaw** *n.* a mistake; an error
  This shirt has a serious **flaw**: The left pocket is missing.

- **fossil** *n.* the preserved remains of a living thing from the distant past
  The scientists found animal **fossils** deep in the ground.

- **mark** *n.* something that can be seen on an object
  I cannot believe my brand-new table already has so many **marks**.

Words and Expressions Refer to the vocabulary to fill in the blanks below. You may need to change the forms of the words.

1 You should not take _____ unless the reward is very great.

2 Adolf Hitler left his _____ on history because of the terrible things he did.

3 Your essay is perfect except for this one _____ : You forgot to put your name on it.

4 The citizens and the politicians _____ how to spend the money given to the city.

5 Ferraris are some of the world's most expensive sports cars and provide _____ _____ performance.

6 The tree looks completely solid, but it is actually _____ .

7 As I child, I enjoyed collecting many different kinds of _____ .

Listening

Now listen to part of a lecture on the topic you just read about.

02-03

Summarizing Read the information below. Use the information to complete the summary of the lecture.

bite marks	nobody knows	could run
able to run	light enough	hollow bones

Main Idea In the lecture, the speaker gives reasons why she thinks Tyrannosaurus rex
_____ .

First Supporting Argument Her first argument deals with the dinosaur's weight. She says
that a Tyrannosaurus had _____ . Therefore, it was
_____ to run without the risk of injury.

Second Supporting Argument For her second argument, the speaker claims that
_____ how large the leg muscles of a Tyrannosaurus rex were.
Moreover, she says that fossils from a fast animal had _____
from a Tyrannosaurus. Due to this, the dinosaur was probably _____
_____ .

Paraphrasing Exercise

Reading The following sentences come from the reading passage summary. Complete each paraphrase with the appropriate words or phrases.

1 The reading passage argues that Tyrannosaurus rex could not run.

→ *The author of the reading passage believes that Tyrannosaurus rex* _____ *to run.*

2 One supporting idea given is that a Tyrannosaurus rex was too heavy to run.

→ *The first supporting argument is that a Tyrannosaurus rex had too much* _____ *to run.*

3 If a Tyrannosaurus rex fell while running, it would have gotten a severe injury.

→ *A Tyrannosaurus rex would have suffered* _____ *if it fell while running.*

4 The second supporting idea is that a Tyrannosaurus rex did not have large enough leg muscles to run.

→ *The next argument states that the leg muscles of a Tyrannosaurus rex were* _____ *for it to run.*

5 But it would have needed muscles larger than fifty percent of its mass to run.

→ *However, its muscles would have needed to be greater than* _____ *weight.*

Listening The following sentences come from the lecture summary. Complete each paraphrase with the appropriate words or phrases.

1 In the lecture, the speaker gives reasons why she thinks Tyrannosaurus rex could run.

→ *The speaker presents arguments* _____ *that Tyrannosaurus rex was able to run.*

2 She says that Tyrannosaurus rex had hollow bones.

→ *The speaker claims that the bones had* _____ *on their insides.*

3 Therefore, it was light enough to run without the risk of injury.

→ *As a result, it was light enough to run without the possibility of* _____ .

4 For her second argument, the speaker claims that nobody knows how large the leg muscles of a Tyrannosaurus rex were.

→ *The speaker's second supporting idea is that* _____ *about the size of a Tyrannosaurus rex's leg muscles.*

5 This means that the dinosaur was probably able to run.

→ *This suggests that the dinosaur was* _____ *of running.*

Tandem Note-Taking

Refer to the summary exercises for the reading and the listening. Paraphrase them to complete the side-by-side notes below. Include only the two points from the reading and the listening that clearly contradict each other.

READING

Main Idea

Tyrannosaurus rex was not able to run.

First Supporting Argument

Tyrannosaurus rex could not run because

it had too much

Supporting Detail

bones were not strong enough   ;

would have been severely

Second Supporting Argument

Tyrannosaurus rex was not able to run

because its leg muscles

Supporting Detail

leg muscles not greater than

LISTENING

Main Idea

Tyrannosaurus rex was able to run.

First Supporting Argument

The bones of a Tyrannosaurus rex were

actually

Supporting Detail

weighed fewer than   ;

could run without the possibility of

Second Supporting Argument

Nobody knows the size of a

Tyrannosaurus rex's

Supporting Detail

bite marks on the fossils of

Use this page to write your response. You have 20 minutes to complete your essay.

Writing Guide	Summarize the points made in the lecture, being sure to explain how they challenge specific arguments made in the reading passage.

First Paragraph ○

State and discuss thesis

_____

_____

_____

Second Paragraph ○

First main idea from reading

Contradiction from lecture

Supporting detail

_____

_____

_____

_____

_____

Third Paragraph ○

Second main idea from reading

Contradiction from lecture

Supporting detail

_____

_____

_____

_____

_____

Fourth Paragraph ○

Conclusion (optional)

_____

_____

_____

_____

✂ **SCAFFOLDING** Here are some useful phrases to help you when you write.

✓ The reading passage and the lecture mainly focus on…

✓ The reading passage argues that…

✓ On the other hand, the speaker believes…

✓ The first argument in the passage is that…

✓ The speaker counters…

✓ The passage's next argument is…

✓ In contrast, the speaker believes…

✓ She provides evidence that…

Read the response carefully to see what makes a response strong.

The reading passage and the lecture mainly focus on whether or not Tyrannosaurus rex could run. The reading passage argues that Tyrannosaurus rex could not run. The speaker challenges this argument in the lecture.

The first argument in the passage is that Tyrannosaurus rex was too heavy to run. The passage explains that Tyrannosaurus rex did not have strong enough bones. The animal also would have been badly injured if it fell while running. The speaker counters these arguments. She says that Tyrannosaurus rex probably had hollow bones. ████████████████ It also would not have gotten hurt if it fell.

The passage's next argument is that Tyrannosaurus rex did not have large enough leg muscles to run. In contrast, the speaker believes this argument is flawed. She feels this way because no one knows how large its leg muscles were. Additionally, scientists have found fossils that had bite marks from Tyrannosaurus rexes. These fossils were from fast animals. Based on this finding, we can assume that Tyrannosaurus rex was a fast runner.

Critical Analysis Refer to the sample response to complete the tasks below.

1   Which of the following sentences is the topic sentence of the third paragraph?
- Ⓐ Additionally, scientists have found fossils that had bite marks from Tyrannosaurus rexes.
- Ⓑ Based on this finding, we can assume that Tyrannosaurus rex was a fast runner.
- Ⓒ The passage's next argument is that Tyrannosaurus rex did not have large enough leg muscles to run.

2   Which of the following sentences would best fit in the blank space in the response?
- Ⓐ This means it would have been light enough to run.
- Ⓑ Scientists have found other dinosaurs with hollow bones.
- Ⓒ The bones of a Tyrannosaurus rex could break very easily.

3   Which word in the response means "**mistaken**"?

4   List the two connecting phrases the writer of the response uses in the third paragraph.

Visiting Historical Sites or Restaurants and Cafés

Question

Some people prefer to visit historical sites in foreign cities. Others prefer to spend time at restaurants and cafés. Which do you prefer? Use specific reasons and examples to support your answer.

Background & Brainstorming

Read the following background information to learn more about the topic.

Visit Historic Rome

Rome is one of the world's greatest cities. Visit Rome and explore some of its many historical sites. Visit the Colosseum, where people once watched gladiators fight. See the Pantheon, the Vatican, and numerous other places. You can learn all about the history of the Roman Republic and the Roman Empire. Find out how people used to live in the past. And see artifacts and artwork from many different time periods in history. You will not regret spending time in Rome and seeing the sights.

Enjoy the Food in Rome

Rome has all kinds of museums and art galleries for people to see. But even better is enjoying the food in Rome. There are plenty of restaurants and cafés for tourists to spend time in. These include five-star restaurants, mom-and-pop establishments, and even places that sell street food. Just relax while you are in Rome and enjoy a good meal. Start up a conversation with the person beside you and meet some real Italians, too. You will love the great meals and drinks in one of the best cities in the world for food.

Understanding the Background Use the background information to complete the sentences below.

1   The archaeologists found some _____ at the dig site.

2   The Renaissance was a great _____ in Europe.

3   Many eating _____ in the city serve seafood.

4   The tourist plan to _____ the museum later in the day.

5   Some of the _____ made by the painters is impressive.

6   Let's have a _____ that includes some traditional Spanish food.

7   There are plenty of _____ to see in France.

8   They saw paintings and sculptures at those _____ last week.

Selecting Ideas Read the sentences below. Decide whether they are about visiting historical sites or spending time at restaurants and cafés. Then, write the sentences on the correct lines below and circle the topic sentences.

- It can be educational to see artifacts from a city's past.

- Some people like learning about the past by going to various places in cities.

- It is fun to sample new foods and to see how people in other places eat.

- Not everyone likes to spend all of their time on their feet.

- A lot about a culture can be learned by studying its history.

- Some people prefer to relax and enjoy a meal when they go somewhere new.

Visiting Historical Sites

Spending Time at Restaurants and Cafés

Generating Ideas Use the ideas you chose in the Selecting Ideas exercise to fill in the blanks below.

Visiting Historical Sites

1 There are _____ in cities that people can see to learn about the past.

2 A person can learn about a country's _____ by studying its past.

3 Examining _____ from a city's past is educational.

Spending Time at Restaurants and Cafés

1 Spending time on _____ is not fun for everyone.

2 Some people prefer to _____ when they visit new cities.

3 _____ is one way to learn about a new city.

Developing Ideas You have now examined the two options. Which of the two do you feel more comfortable developing into an essay? Explain why you feel this way.

Some people prefer to visit historical sites in foreign cities. Others prefer to spend time at restaurants and cafés. Which do you prefer? Use specific reasons and examples to support your answer.

Visiting Historical Sites

Thesis Statement

A lot of people like to learn about the past by going to historical sites in cities.

First Supporting Idea

Supporting Example

Second Supporting Idea

Supporting Example

Conclusion

Spending Time at Restaurants and Cafés

Thesis Statement

Many people enjoy spending time at restaurants and cafés when they visit foreign cities.

First Supporting Idea

Supporting Example

Second Supporting Idea

Supporting Example

Conclusion

Writing

Use this page to write your response. You have 30 minutes to complete your essay.

First Paragraph ○

State and discuss thesis

_____

_____

_____

Second Paragraph ○

First main supporting idea

Supporting detail

Example

_____

_____

_____

_____

Third Paragraph ○

Second main supporting idea

Supporting detail

Example

_____

_____

_____

_____

Fourth Paragraph ○

Conclusion

_____

_____

_____

_____

_____

✂ SCAFFOLDING Here are some useful phrases to help you when you write.

✓ Some people enjoy…

✓ As for me, I prefer to…

✓ My first reason is that…

✓ In some places…

✓ I also (do not) enjoy spending all of my time…

✓ But if I…

✓ In addition, I can…

✓ It is easy to…

Read the response carefully to see what makes a response strong.

People today travel to foreign countries quite frequently. Some people enjoy visiting historical sites on their trips to foreign cities. As for me, however, I prefer to spend most of my time at restaurants and cafés.

My first reason is that I love to try new foods anytime that I visit a new city. People in most cities have their own unique food cultures. In some places, spicy food is popular. In others, vegetable dishes or seafood dishes may be more common. Some cities also have unique cooking methods that are used. I love to try all of these foods and different cooking methods. For me, that is the highlight of my trip.

I also do not enjoy spending all of my time on my feet. It can be tiring walking from place to place to see the sights. But if I spend time at restaurants and cafés, I can have a more relaxing trip. In addition, I can meet natives more easily when I am at restaurants and cafés. It is easy to start a conversation with a person nearby. That way, I can talk to real natives of the country and possible even make new friends.

In my experience, it is much better to spend time at restaurants and cafés than to visit historical sites when I go to a foreign city.

Critical Analysis Refer to the sample response to complete the tasks below.

1   Which of the following sentences is the thesis statement of the response?
   Ⓐ As for me, however, I prefer to spend most of my time at restaurants and cafés.
   Ⓑ I also do not enjoy spending all of my time on my feet.
   Ⓒ I love to try all of these foods and different cooking methods.

2   Which sentence below is closest in meaning to the underlined sentence?
   Ⓐ Yet I prefer to relax when I am going to a restaurant.
   Ⓑ But I can relax more by going to places where I can eat.
   Ⓒ However, I like to spend time at restaurants and cafés.

3   List the two connecting words the writer uses in the third paragraph.

Part B

Agriculture: **The Pros and Cons of Using Fertilizer**

🎯 **Vocabulary** Take a few moments to review the vocabulary items that will appear in this task.

- **crop** *n.* a plant that is grown to eat or use in other ways
  The farmer's rice **crop** is growing well this year.

- **fertilizer** *n.* something added to make land more productive
  This **fertilizer** helps plants grow very well.

- **soil** *n.* ground; dirt; earth
  Plant the seeds in the **soil** and water them.

- **yield** *n.* a quantity or amount produced
  The wheat **yield** will be lower than normal due to the weather.

- **nutrient** *n.* something that promotes growth and good health
  The field needs more **nutrients** to be productive.

- **fertile** *adj.* capable of being productive
  The land is **fertile**, so plants grow well on it.

- **multiple** *adj.* many
  He will plant seeds in **multiple** fields this weekend.

- **annually** *adv.* each year; once a year
  The farmers **annually** plant their crops in spring.

- **harvest** *v.* to gather ripe crops in a field
  When the farmers **harvest** corn, they use machines.

- **starvation** *n.* the act of dying from a lack of food
  Starvation is a big problem in some poor countries.

Words and Expressions Refer to the vocabulary to fill in the blanks below. You may need to change the forms of the words.

1 The ground in the desert is not very _____.

2 _____ is a huge problem in some African countries.

3 There are _____ problems that we must solve.

4 The tractor is preparing the _____ for spring planting.

5 The _____ in the fields are growing very well.

6 _____ like nitrogen are necessary for plants to grow well.

7 It can take days to _____ crops at a large farm.

8 By adding _____, he can make more corn grow in the fields.

9 The _____ is not as big as it was last year.

10 He has a party on his birthday _____.

Reading

Read the passage carefully. Try to understand what the main argument of the passage is. You have 3 minutes to read.

Farmers around the world grow many different crops. Most of these farmers have one thing in common. They almost all add fertilizer to the soil in their fields. Fertilizer can provide a number of benefits.

First, fertilizer can increase the crop yield for farmers. There are a variety of types of fertilizer. They add nutrients such as nitrogen, potassium, and phosphorus to the soil. These make the soil more fertile. That lets farmers grow more crops. Studies have shown that in some places, fertilizer has increased the yield of corn fields by more than forty percent. It can also make wheat fields more productive by sixty percent.

There is a second advantage to using fertilizer. It enables some farmers to get multiple crop yields each year. For instance, in some places, farmers get two crops of rice annually. In other places, farmers may grow grain first and then vegetables after they harvest the grain. They are able to do this because there are enough nutrients in the soil thanks to the fertilizer. As a result, more food is produced on an annual basis. This provides people with more calories and helps reduce the threat of starvation in places.

Summarizing Read the information below. Use the information to complete the summary for the reading passage.

enough nutrients	the crop yield	threat of starvation
using fertilizer	corn and wheat	many benefits

Main Idea The reading passage deals with the issue of _____ . The reading passage states that it provides _____ .

First Supporting Argument The passage first argues that fertilizer can increase _____ for farmers. It adds nutrients such as nitrogen, potassium, and phosphorous to the soil. As a result, the yields of crops like _____ increase.

Second Supporting Argument Next, the passage explains that fertilizer lets farmers get multiple crop yields every year. Because there are _____ in the soil, farmers can get two crops of the same or different plants. This helps reduce the _____ .

- **propose** *v.* to suggest
  I **propose** that we try a new method this year.

- **damage** *v.* to harm
  Pollution is **damaging** the environment in many places.

- **excessive** *adj.* going beyond what is usual or necessary
  The **excessive** noise is bothering everyone.

- **decline** *v.* to go down; to become less in number or amount
  The ability of the land to grow plants is **declining**.

- **infertile** *adj.* unable to produce anything
  Only a few small plants are growing on the **infertile** land.

- **virtually** *adv.* nearly; almost
  There is **virtually** no water in the pond now.

- **rotate** *v.* to make something go through a cycle of changes
  Rotate the object to let each part of it get enough sun.

- **remove** *v.* to take out or away
  Please **remove** the dirty clothes from the floor.

- **replace** *v.* to provide one thing as a substitute for another
  He **replaced** the old bricks in the wall with new ones.

- **fallow** *adj.* not in use; plowed but unseeded, as in a field
  They will leave this field **fallow** for the entire year.

Words and Expressions Refer to the vocabulary to fill in the blanks below. You may need to change the forms of the words.

1 As the temperature _____, the weather gets colder.

2 The airplane propeller _____ and helps the plane fly.

3 The wall _____ the car when the car hit it.

4 This field will lie _____ so that it does not lose more nutrients.

5 There is _____ nothing she can do to help him.

6 Please _____ a new way to solve the problem.

7 They will _____ the weeds from the garden.

8 _____ land cannot produce any crops.

9 _____ all of the broken parts with new ones.

10 The _____ rain falling is causing flooding.

Listening

Now listen to part of a lecture on the topic you just read about.

02-04

Summarizing Read the information below. Use the information to complete the summary for the lecture.

take care of it	become infertile	rotate the crops
the three-field system	harmful to soil	damage the soil

Main Idea The lecturer explains that fertilizer can be _____. He adds that there are other ways to _____.

First Supporting Argument The lecturer first argues that too much fertilizer can _____. This takes place after around thirty years. When the soil is damaged, the land can _____.

Second Supporting Argument The lecturer next mentions that crop rotation can help the soil instead of adding fertilizer. Farmers _____ they grow in their fields by using _____. Then, the soil can become healthier.

Paraphrasing Exercise

Reading The following sentences come from the reading passage summary. Complete each paraphrase with the appropriate words or phrases.

1 The reading passage deals with the issue of using fertilizer.

→ *The reading passage deals with the _____ of using fertilizer.*

2 The passage first argues that fertilizer can increase the crop yield for farmers.

→ *The passage first argues that fertilizer can _____ the crop yield for farmers.*

3 It adds nutrients such as nitrogen, potassium, and phosphorous to the soil.

→ *It adds nutrients such as nitrogen, potassium, and phosphorous to the _____ .*

4 Next, the passage explains that fertilizer lets farmers get multiple crop yields every year.

→ *Next, the passage explains that fertilizer allows farmers to _____ more than one crop every year.*

5 This helps reduce the threat of starvation.

→ *This helps _____ the threat of starvation.*

Listening The following sentences come from the lecture summary. Complete each paraphrase with the appropriate words or phrases.

1 The lecturer explains that fertilizer can be harmful to soil.

→ *The lecturer states that fertilizer can be _____ for soil.*

2 The lecturer first argues that too much fertilizer can damage the soil.

→ *His first argument is that using too much fertilizer can _____ problems for the soil.*

3 When the soil is damaged, the land can become infertile.

→ *When the soil is harmed, the land can become _____ .*

4 The lecturer next mentions that crop rotation can help the soil instead of adding fertilizer.

→ *The lecturer next mentions that crop rotation can help the soil _____ adding fertilizer.*

5 Farmers rotate the crops they grow in their fields by using the three-field system.

→ *Farmers _____ the crops they grow in their fields by using the three-field system.*

Tandem Note-Taking

Refer to the summary exercises for the reading and the listening. Paraphrase them to complete the side-by-side notes below. Include only the two points from the reading and the listening that clearly contradict each other.

READING

Main Idea

Fertilizer provides many benefits to fields.

First Supporting Argument

Fertilizer can improve

Supporting Detail

adds nutrients such as

;

corn and wheat

Second Supporting Argument

Farmers can get

Supporting Detail

soil has enough nutrients; can get

; reduces

LISTENING

Main Idea

Fertilizer can be harmful to the soil.

First Supporting Argument

Too much fertilizer can cause

Supporting Detail

damage takes place over thirty years;

land becomes

Second Supporting Argument

Crop rotation is a better way to

Supporting Detail

rotate crops grown in fields; use

;

soil becomes

Writing

Use this page to write your response. You have 20 minutes to complete your essay.

Writing Guide

Summarize the points made in the lecture, being sure to explain how they cast doubt on specific points made in the reading passage.

First Paragraph ○

State and discuss thesis

_____
_____
_____

Second Paragraph ○

First main idea from lecture

Contradiction from reading

Supporting detail

_____
_____
_____
_____
_____

Third Paragraph ○

Second main idea from lecture

Contradiction from reading

Supporting detail

_____
_____
_____
_____
_____

Fourth Paragraph ○

Conclusion (optional)

_____
_____
_____
_____

✕ SCAFFOLDING
Here are some useful phrases to help you when you write.

✓ The author of the reading passage argues…

✓ Meanwhile, the lecturer argues…

✓ The lecturer begins by stating that…

✓ The lecturer therefore believes that…

✓ This argument goes against…

✓ For his second argument, the lecturer discusses…

✓ To illustrate this, the lecturer talks about…

✓ This argument suggests that…

Sample Response

Read the response carefully to see what makes a response strong.

The author of the reading passage argues in favor of using fertilizer in fields. But the lecturer believes that using other farming methods is better.

The lecturer begins by stating that too much fertilizer in a field can be harmful. He explains that fertilizer can affect the long-term health of the soil. After around thirty years, the land will be damaged. So the number of crops that can grow on the land will decline. This argument goes against the one in the reading passage. The passage claims that fertilizer can increase crop yields a tremendous amount.

For his second argument, the lecturer discusses the benefits of crop rotation. He covers the three-field system. In this method, farmers plant wheat in one field, peas in another, and nothing in the last one. Then, farmers rotate the fields each year. This helps the soil become healthy. This casts doubt on the argument in the reading passage. It states that farmers can get multiple crop yields in their fields each year thanks to the use of fertilizer.

Critical Analysis Refer to the sample response to complete the tasks below.

1   Which of the following sentences is the topic sentence of the second paragraph?
   Ⓐ This argument goes against the one in the reading passage.
   Ⓑ The passage claims that fertilizer can increase crop yields a tremendous amount.
   Ⓒ The lecturer begins by stating that too much fertilizer in a field can be harmful.

2   Which sentence below is closest in meaning to the underlined sentence?
   Ⓐ Then, farmers plans their crops in their fields each year.
   Ⓑ Then, farmers change the crops they plant in the fields annually.
   Ⓒ Then, farmers think about which plants to grow in their fields each year.

3   Which word in the response means "**very much**"?

4   List the connecting word the writer of the response uses in the third paragraph.

Students Should Not Have Part-Time Jobs

? Question

Do you agree or disagree with the following statement? Students should not have part-time jobs while attending university. Use specific reasons and examples to support your answer.

▌Background & Brainstorming

Read the following background information to learn more about the topic.

The Daily Bugle: Editorial Page

I am writing this letter to complain about the college's cancelation of its part-time jobs for students. Many students like me want to earn money and live independently. We do not want to rely on our parents for money. We also want to learn time-management skills. Having a job would teach us how to balance work time with study time. Working part time would also give us practical job skills. In conclusion, I urge the university to reconsider its policy on part-time jobs for students.

Joshua Elder, Junior

As a professor, I agree with the university's decision to get rid of its part-time jobs for students. For one, the students have too much schoolwork to work at a part-time job. In my experience, working students usually have lower grades than students who do not work. Besides, many part-time jobs do not pay much money. Even students with jobs still have to get money from their parents sometimes. Lastly, part-time jobs can cause students unnecessary stress. Based on these drawbacks, the students are better off not being able to work.

Professor Thomas Mack, Political Science Department

Understanding the Background Use the background information to complete the sentences below.

1 A lot of college students want to _____ and live independently.

2 Students can get unnecessary _____ from part-time jobs.

3 With jobs, students do not need to _____ their parents for money.

4 Part-time jobs teach students how to _____ work time with study time.

5 Students who work often have _____ than students who do not work.

6 Part-time jobs usually do not pay _____ .

7 Most college students have too much _____ to work at any part-time jobs.

8 Part-time jobs can give students _____ job skills.

Read the sentences below. Decide whether they agree or disagree with the given statement. Then, write the sentences on the correct lines below and circle the topic sentences.

- Students with jobs learn how to make good use of their time.

- Most part-time jobs do not pay very high salaries.

- Having a part-time job is a great way for students to solve their money problems.

- Having a part-time job can cause college students a lot of problems.

- Students with jobs often have worse grades than students who do not.

- Part-time jobs also give students practical job skills.

Agree

_____

_____

_____

Disagree

_____

_____

_____

Generating Ideas Use the ideas you chose in the Selecting Ideas exercise to fill in the blanks below.

Agree

1 Part-time jobs sometimes create _____ for college students.

2 Students who work cannot focus on their _____ and often get worse grades.

3 Salaries at part-time jobs are usually not _____ .

Disagree

1 Students can fix their _____ by having a part-time job.

2 Students learn how to make _____ of their time by having a part-time job.

3 Doing a part-time job can teach students practical _____ .

Developing Ideas You have now examined the two options. Which of the two do you feel more comfortable developing into an essay? Explain why you feel this way.

Planning

Do you agree or disagree with the following statement? Students should not have part-time jobs while attending university. Use specific reasons and examples to support your answer.

Agree

Thesis Statement

Having a part-time job sometimes creates problems for college students.

First Supporting Idea

Supporting Example

Second Supporting Idea

Supporting Example

Conclusion

Disagree

Thesis Statement

Part-time jobs allow students to fix their money problems.

First Supporting Idea

Supporting Example

Second Supporting Idea

Supporting Example

Conclusion

Writing

Use this page to write your response. You have 30 minutes to complete your essay.

Writing Guide

Do you agree or disagree with the following statement? Students should not have part-time jobs while attending university. Use specific reasons and examples to support your answer.

First Paragraph ○

State and discuss thesis

_____
_____
_____

Second Paragraph ○

First main supporting idea

Supporting detail

Example

_____
_____
_____
_____

Third Paragraph ○

Second main supporting idea

Supporting detail

Example

_____
_____
_____
_____

Fourth Paragraph ○

Conclusion

_____
_____
_____
_____

✂ **SCAFFOLDING** Here are some useful phrases to help you when you write.

✓ One of the main concerns for university students is…

✓ To correct this problem, I feel that…

✓ To begin with, part-time jobs teach students…

✓ The reason is that her part-time job taught her…

✓ Part-time jobs are also beneficial because…

✓ For instance, my older brother did not…

✓ My sister, on the other hand, is…

✓ However, I feel that college students…

Read the response carefully to see what makes a response strong.

One of the main concerns for university students is money. Many students get scholarships and loans to pay for classes. However, they do not cover everyday costs such as food and transportation. To correct this problem, I feel that college students should be able to have part-time jobs.

To begin with, part-time jobs teach students to manage their time more efficiently. If students have to work and study, then they must learn to use their time effectively. In college, my sister worked part time at a coffee shop. She worked in the morning, attended classes in the afternoon, and studied in the evening. My sister had a busy schedule. Even so, she was still able to get straight A's. Today, she is highly successful. The reason is that her part-time job taught her how to use her time well in college.

Part-time jobs are also beneficial because they allow students to learn practical job skills. **1** Jobs teach students about earning money. Students also learn about taking orders from supervisors. **2** For instance, my older brother did not have a job in college. **3** Like my sister, he was a good student. Unlike my sister, he never learned how to manage his money. He still has trouble saving his money to this day. My sister, on the other hand, is very good with her money.

Some people may believe that college students should only study. However, I feel that college students greatly benefit from having part-time jobs.

Critical Analysis Refer to the sample response to complete the tasks below.

1 Which of the following sentences is the topic sentence of the third paragraph?

   (A) Students also learn about taking orders from supervisors.

   (B) For instance, my older brother did not have a job in college.

   (C) Part-time jobs are also beneficial because they allow students to learn practical job skills.

2 Where should the following sentence be added to improve the response?

These are important life lessons that are not taught in college.

   (A) **1**

   (B) **2**

   (C) **3**

3 List the connecting word the writer uses in the last paragraph.

Part B

Archaeology: **The Builders of Stonehenge**

🎯 **Vocabulary** Take a few moments to review the vocabulary items that will appear in this task.

- **countless** *adj.* too many to be counted; numerous
  There are **countless** stars in the night sky.

- **site** *n.* the place or setting of something
  We need to choose a new **site** for our office.

- **construct** *v.* to create by putting together parts; to build
  The city is **constructing** a new city hall building.

- **suggest** *v.* to offer up an idea or something to think about
  My mother **suggested** that I become a singer.

- **descended** *v.* to be related to
  My family is **descended** from Thomas Jefferson.

- **document** *n.* a piece of writing that provides information
  To get your driver's license, you must provide **documents** showing your place of birth.

- **layout** *n.* the way something is organized; a design
  This map shows the **layout** of the castle.

- **ritual** *n.* a set of acts done for religious reasons
  Praying is a **ritual** done in many religions.

- **summer solstice** *n.* the time when the sun is farthest from the equator
  The **summer solstice** occurs every year on June 21.

- **century** *n.* a period of one hundred years
  Very few people live longer than a **century**.

Words and Expressions Refer to the vocabulary to fill in the blanks below. You may need to change the forms of the words.

1 Having a wedding is a common _____ when people get married.

2 How do you _____ that we improve our customer service?

3 Our company is currently _____ a new factory.

4 The longest day of the year happens during the _____ .

5 Many Chinese people are _____ from Mongolians.

6 I do not like the _____ of this apartment.

7 We are now living in the twenty-first _____ .

8 This _____ proves that I am innocent.

9 The military has chosen a new _____ for the army base.

10 You can solve this puzzle in a _____ number of ways.

Reading

Read the passage carefully. Try to understand what the main argument of the passage is. You have 3 minutes to read.

There have been countless debates about Stonehenge over the years. Although people are not sure who first used Stonehenge, many agree that the Druids used the site for hundreds of years. It is therefore likely that the Druids constructed Stonehenge.

The first piece of evidence suggesting that the Druids built Stonehenge relates to their history. The Druids are descended from the Celts. The Celts were among the first people to live in England. For this reason, the Druids were probably the first people to live around the Stonehenge building site. Indeed, one document from the seventeenth century states that Stonehenge was constructed to pay respect to the Celtic queen Boudicca. From this, it is likely that the Druids were the builders of Stonehenge.

Additionally, the layout of Stonehenge perfectly fits with Druid rituals. Tracking the movements of the sun and the moon is an important part of Druid beliefs. Stonehenge tracks the points where the sun and the moon rise and set. This would have allowed the Druids to use the site to follow events taking place in the sky. Due to this fact, Druids celebrated the summer solstice at the site for several centuries. This strongly suggests that Stonehenge was created by the Druids.

Summarizing Read the information below. Use the information to complete the summary for the reading passage.

first people	follow events	perfectly fits
Celtic queen Boudicca	rise and set	Druids constructed

Main Idea In the reading passage, the author gives two arguments to explain that the _____ Stonehenge.

First Supporting Argument For the opening argument, the author states that the Druids were probably the _____ to live around Stonehenge. The writer supports this by explaining that Stonehenge was constructed to pay respect to the _____ .

Second Supporting Argument The next argument is that Stonehenge's layout _____ with Druid rituals. Stonehenge tracks the points where the sun and the moon _____ . It is therefore likely that the Druids used the site to _____ occurring in the sky.

- **common** *adj.* happening very often; usual
  Seeing students in this restaurant is **common** in the afternoons.

- **structure** *n.* something constructed, such as a building
  The hurricane damaged all the **structures** along the coast.

- **carbon dating** *n.* a scientific process that measures how old an object is
  The scientists used **carbon dating** to determine how old the bones were.

- **seem** *v.* to appear to be true or likely
  It **seems** like it is going to rain today.

- **ceremony** *n.* an act or set of acts done in a certain way
  Most high schools have graduation **ceremonies** at the end of the year.

- **worship** *v.* to love or respect something deeply
  The ancient Egyptians **worshiped** the sun.

- **marsh** *n.* land that is wet and soft all the time
  Many alligators and frogs live in **marshes**.

- **manmade** *adj.* made by human beings instead of nature; artificial
  Cotton is a natural material while polyester is **manmade**.

- **recently** *adv.* newly; lately
  I have **recently** started studying karate.

Words and Expressions Refer to the vocabulary to fill in the blanks below. You may need to change the forms of the words.

1 Maria _____ older than she really is.

2 This lake may look natural, but it is actually _____.

3 We held a _____ to honor the soldiers that died.

4 The church is the oldest standing _____ on the island.

5 Crime rates have _____ gone up after falling for many years.

6 According to _____, the tree is about 4,000 years old.

7 It is _____ for snow to fall in the mountains throughout the year.

8 The oil spill damaged many of the _____ near the ocean.

9 Most religious people _____ a god.

Listening

Now listen to part of a lecture on the topic you just read about.

02-05

Summarizing Read the information below. Use the information to complete the summary for the lecture.

for rituals	manmade places	2,000 years
long connection	did not build	carbon dating

Main Idea The professor gives reasons to explain why the Druids _____ Stonehenge.

First Supporting Argument To start off, the professor explains that scientists used _____ to figure out how old Stonehenge is. They found that its structures were built more than _____ before the Celts went to England.

Second Supporting Argument The professor then goes over the debate about the use of the site _____. She believes that the Druids did not worship in _____. This means that the Druids did not have a _____ with Stonehenge.

Paraphrasing Exercise

Reading   The following sentences come from the reading passage summary. Complete each paraphrase with the appropriate words or phrases.

1   In the reading passage, the author gives two arguments to explain that the Druids constructed Stonehenge.

→ *The reading passage presents two reasons explaining that the Druids _____ Stonehenge.*

2   For the opening argument, the author states that the Druids were probably the first people to live around Stonehenge.

→ *The first _____ is that the Druids were probably the first people to stay around Stonehenge.*

3   The writer supports this by explaining that Stonehenge was constructed to pay respect to the Celtic queen Boudicca.

→ *To _____ this idea, the author states that Stonehenge was built to honor the Celtic queen Boudicca.*

4   The next argument is that Stonehenge's layout perfectly fits with Druid rituals.

→ *The second argument is that the _____ of Stonehenge matches Druid religious acts.*

5   It is therefore likely that they used the site to follow events occurring in the sky for centuries.

→ *Therefore, the Druids probably used the location to _____ events happening in the sky.*

Listening   The following sentences come from the lecture summary. Complete each paraphrase with the appropriate words or phrases.

1   The professor gives reasons to explain that the Druids did not build Stonehenge.

→ *The professor _____ to explain that the Druids did not construct Stonehenge.*

2   To start off, the professor explains that scientists used carbon dating to figure out how old Stonehenge is.

→ *To begin with, the professor says that researchers used carbon dating to determine the _____ of Stonehenge.*

3   They found that the structures were built more than 2,000 years before the Celts came to England.

→ *They _____ that the site was completed more than 2,000 years before the Celts arrived in England.*

4   She believes that Druids would not have worshiped in manmade places.

→ *She feels that the Druids would not have worshiped in _____ .*

5   This means that the Druids probably did not have a long connection with Stonehenge.

→ *Therefore, it is _____ that the Druids had a long connection with Stonehenge.*

Tandem Note-Taking

Refer to the summary exercises for the reading and the listening. Paraphrase them to complete the side-by-side notes below. Include only the two points from the reading and the listening that clearly contradict each other.

READING

Main Idea

The Druids constructed Stonehenge.

First Supporting Argument

The Druids were among the first people

to

Supporting Detail

was built to honor

Second Supporting Argument

The design of Stonehenge matches

Supporting Detail

tracks events happening

LISTENING

Main Idea

Stonehenge was not built by the Druids.

First Supporting Argument

Scientists used carbon dating to

Supporting Detail

completed nearly 2,000 years before

Second Supporting Argument

The Druids would not have

Supporting Detail

actually worshiped in

Writing

Use this page to write your response. You have 20 minutes to complete your essay.

First Paragraph ○

State and discuss thesis

_____
_____
_____

Second Paragraph ○

First main idea from lecture

Contradiction from reading

Supporting detail

_____
_____
_____
_____
_____

Third Paragraph ○

Second main idea from lecture

Contradiction from reading

Supporting detail

_____
_____
_____
_____
_____

Fourth Paragraph ○

Conclusion (optional)

_____
_____
_____
_____

✗SCAFFOLDING Here are some useful phrases to help you when you write.

✓ The reading passage and the lecture present…

✓ The author of the passage argues…

✓ The professor, on the other hand, believes…

✓ For her first argument, the professor talks about…

✓ This argument calls into question the one given in…

✓ The text stated that…

✓ The professor's second argument deals with…

✓ In the reading passage, however, it is argued…

Read the response carefully to see what makes a response strong.

The reading passage and the lecture present different opinions about the construction of Stonehenge. The author of the passage argues that the Druids built Stonehenge. The professor, on the other hand, believes they did not build it.

For her first argument, the professor talks about the age of Stonehenge. She explains that scientists have used carbon dating to determine the age of the structure. They found that Stonehenge was built about 2,000 years before the Celts first came to England. This argument calls into the question the one given in the reading passage. The text states that the Druids were the first to build Stonehenge.

The professor's second argument deals with Stonehenge as a place of worship. Some believe that the Druids used Stonehenge as a place of worship. However, the Druids usually worshiped in forests and other natural places. They probably did not use artificial places such as Stonehenge. In the reading passage, however, it is argued that the Druids used Stonehenge to track the movements of the sun and the moon.

Critical Analysis Refer to the sample response to complete the tasks below.

1 Which of the following sentences is the transition sentence of the second paragraph?
   Ⓐ The text states that the Druids were the first to build Stonehenge.
   Ⓑ For her first argument, the professor talks about the age of Stonehenge.
   Ⓒ This argument calls into the question the one given in the reading passage.

2 Which of the following sentences is the topic sentence of the third paragraph?
   Ⓐ In the reading passage, however, it is argued that the Druids used Stonehenge to track the movements of the sun and moon.
   Ⓑ The professor's second argument deals with Stonehenge as a place of worship.
   Ⓒ However, the Druids usually worshiped in forests and other natural places.

3 Which word in the response means "**manmade**"?

4 List the connecting phrase the writer of the response uses in the first paragraph.

Parents Should Make Decisions for Their Children

? Question

Do you agree or disagree with the following statement? Parents should make important decisions for their children. Use specific reasons and examples to support your answer.

Background & Brainstorming

Reead the following background information to learn more about the topic.

In Favor

Children should not be allowed to make important decisions. For one, children are too young to make serious decisions. They simply do not have enough knowledge and experience to make the best decisions. Children also think only in the short term. They often fail to think about the long-term effects of their choices. Furthermore, parents almost always try to do what is best for their children. Few parents would make bad decisions on purpose.

In Opposition

Children benefit from being able to make their own important decisions in many ways. One reason is that it gives them experience in making decisions. As adults, children will have to make many important decisions. Additionally, children who make their own decisions mature more quickly. They learn how making decisions can affect their lives. They also understand the consequences of making bad decisions. Finally, important decisions can change the lives of children. Therefore, children should be able to make these decisions themselves.

Understanding the Background Use the background information to complete the sentences below.

1 Children do not have enough _____ to make the best decisions.

2 Having children make _____ also has its drawbacks.

3 Making important decisions allows children to _____ more quickly.

4 Most children do not think of the _____ of their decisions.

5 Making decisions teaches children how the choices they make _____ .

6 Parents almost always attempt to do _____ for their children.

7 Children cannot make good decisions because they are _____ .

8 Important decisions can _____ of children.

- Children can benefit from making important decisions on their own.

- Children often do not think about the long-term effects of their choices.

- The lives of children can greatly change because of important decisions.

- Children do not posses enough experience and knowledge to make proper decisions.

- Allowing children to make important decisions has serious drawbacks.

- Children gain experience making decisions at a young age.

Agree

Disagree

Generating Ideas Use the ideas you chose in the Selecting Ideas exercise to fill in the blanks below.

Agree

1 There are _____ to allowing children to make important decisions.

2 Making important decisions requires _____ that children lack.

3 Children usually fail to think about the _____ of their decisions.

Disagree

1 Allowing children to make important decisions _____ them.

2 Important decisions can _____ the lives of children.

3 Children can _____ by making decisions when they are young.

Developing Ideas You have now examined the two options. Which of the two do you feel more comfortable developing into an essay? Explain why you feel this way.

Do you agree or disagree with the following statement? Parents should make important decisions for their children. Use specific reasons and examples to support your answer.

Agree

Thesis Statement

Allowing children to make important decisions has serious drawbacks.

First Supporting Idea

Supporting Example

Second Supporting Idea

Supporting Example

Conclusion

Disagree

Thesis Statement

Children can greatly benefit from making important decisions.

First Supporting Idea

Supporting Example

Second Supporting Idea

Supporting Example

Conclusion

Writing

Use this page to write your response. You have 30 minutes to complete your essay.

Writing Guide

Do you agree or disagree with the following statement? Parents should make important decisions for their children. Use specific reasons and examples to support your answer.

First Paragraph ○

State and discuss thesis

_____

_____

_____

Second Paragraph ○

First main supporting idea

Supporting detail

Example

_____

_____

_____

_____

_____

Third Paragraph ○

Second main supporting idea

Supporting detail

Example

_____

_____

_____

_____

_____

Fourth Paragraph ○

Conclusion

_____

_____

_____

_____

✂**SCAFFOLDING** Here are some useful phrases to help you when you write.

✓ A central part of growing up is…

✓ It is for this reason that I agree/disagree that…

✓ For one, children who are allowed to make decisions…

✓ One reason children should not make decisions is…

✓ In contrast, my cousin had…

✓ When I was young, my parents…

✓ In the end, I decided to…

✓ In conclusion, I think parents/children should make…

Read the response carefully to see what makes a response strong.

A central part of growing up is learning how to make decisions. Because of this, I disagree that parents need to make decisions for their children. Children who make their own decisions will mature more quickly. They also have more control over their lives.

For one, children who are allowed to make decisions mature more quickly. These children learn the consequences of making bad decisions. This leads them to make better decisions at younger ages. For example, one of my cousin's friends had parents that made all of her decisions for her. By the time she got into college, she had no experience making decisions. **1** In contrast, my cousin had a lot of experience making decisions. **2** His time in college was much better as a result. **3**

Furthermore, children should make decisions that affect their lives. When I was young, my parents allowed me to choose whether or not I wanted to study in the United States. I had to think about the reasons for and against this. In the end, I decided to study in the U.S. I did this because I knew it would help me improve my English. If my parents had made this decision for me, then maybe I would not have studied very hard in America. By making the decision myself, I was able to think critically about my future.

In conclusion, I do not think that parents should make important decisions for their children.

Critical Analysis Refer to the sample response to complete the tasks below.

1   Which of the following sentences is the supporting example from the third paragraph?
   (A) By making the decision myself, I was able to think critically about my future.
   (B) I did this because I knew it would help me improve my English.
   (C) Furthermore, children should make decisions that affect their lives.

2   Where should the following sentence be added to improve the response?
   This caused her to make many bad decisions and to get into trouble.
   (A) **1**
   (B) **2**
   (C) **3**

3   List the three connecting phrases the writer uses in the second paragraph.

Part B

Environmental Science: **Electric Vehicles vs. Gasoline-Powered Vehicles**

🎯 **Vocabulary** Take a few moments to review the vocabulary items that will appear in this task.

- **pollutant** *n.* anything that makes the land, air, or water dirty

  There are so many **pollutants** in the ocean.

- **release** *v.* to let go; to send out

  The factory **releases** too much pollution into the atmosphere.

- **battery** *n.* a device that can store energy

  The **battery** of the phone is almost out.

- **recharge** *v.* to charge again with electricity

  It can take a couple of hours to completely **recharge** an electric vehicle.

- **efficient** *adj.* performing in the best way possible

  The employee is **efficient** and always does a good job at work.

- **maintenance** *n.* the act of keeping something such as a machine in good condition

  Proper **maintenance** is necessary to keep the machine working.

- **internal combustion engine** *n.* an engine that runs when fuel is burned

  Most cars today use an **internal combustion engine**.

- **break down** *v.* to stop working; to fail

  The engine will **break down** if it has no oil.

- **mechanic** *n.* a person who fixes vehicles

  I took my car to the **mechanic** when it stopped running.

- **repair** *v.* to fix something that is broken

  He is trying to **repair** the car's motor.

Words and Expressions Refer to the vocabulary to fill in the blanks below. You may need to change the forms of the words.

1   This is the most _____ way to solve the problem.

2   The car requires yearly _____ on its engine.

3   Too much smoke is _____ by the factory.

4   Two people are trying to _____ the broken machine.

5   It takes thirty minutes to _____ this smartphone.

6   An _____ needs gas to run.

7   The _____ knows how to fix most kinds of trucks.

8   It is against the law to put _____ into the air.

9   The machine will _____ unless you stop using it.

10 The laptop _____ can run for about two hours.

◼ Reading

Read the passage carefully. Try to understand what the main argument of the passage is. You have 3 minutes to read.

In recent years, electric vehicles, or EVs, have become common. They do not use gasoline-powered engines. Instead, they are powered by lithium-ion batteries. People buy them for various reasons.

First, EVs are good for the environment. Unlike gasoline-powered engines, the engines of EVs do not produce any pollutants. EVs also do not release clouds of smoke or burn gas. As a result, the vehicles do not harm the environment. While their batteries need to be recharged, that does not require much energy because EV batteries are energy efficient. Overall, EVs are much better for the environment than cars that use gas.

A second advantage is that EVs do not require much maintenance. Gas-powered cars have internal combustion engines. These engines have a large number of moving parts. These parts frequently break down. The engines must also undergo maintenance or be replaced with great frequency. EVs, on the other hand, have motors that need very little maintenance. The cars do not break down often either. Thus, owners of EVs do not have to spend much money paying mechanics to repair their cars.

Summarizing Read the information below. Use the information to complete the summary for the reading passage.

energy efficient	many good reasons	pay mechanics
for the environment	no pollutants	much maintenance

Main Idea The reading passage argues that people have _____ to buy electric vehicles.

First Supporting Argument To begin with, the passage explains that electric vehicles are good _____. The reason is that they produce _____. Their batteries are also _____. And they are better for the environment than cars that use gas.

Second Supporting Argument The passage then argues that electric vehicles do not require _____. Unlike internal combustion engines, which often break down, the engines of EVs do not. So people do not have to _____ to repair their cars.

⊙ Vocabulary Take a few moments to review the vocabulary items that will appear in this task.

- **emission** *n.* something that is released into the air
  The **emissions** are causing a lot of air pollution.

- **mining** *n.* the act of digging in the earth for rocks or minerals
  Mining is often a very dangerous job.

- **terrible** *adj.* very bad
  I have a **terrible** headache now.

- **poison** *v.* to kill or injure by using a harmful substance
  The factory is **poisoning** the land with its harmful emissions.

- **power plant** *n.* a place that creates electricity
  The **power plant** makes enough energy for the entire city.

- **require** *v.* to need
  It **requires** hard work to learn a new language.

- **average** *adj.* typical; common; usual
  The **average** person works around eight hours a day.

- **replacement** *n.* a substitute for a person or thing
  We need some **replacement** parts to fix the motor.

- **inexpensive** *adj.* cheap; not costing a lot of money
  The gold necklace looks nice and is **inexpensive**.

- **fee** *n.* a payment for a professional service
  Doctors' **fees** cost a lot of money at times.

Words and Expressions Refer to the vocabulary to fill in the blanks below. You may need to change the forms of the words.

1 The shirt is high in quality but also _____.

2 The weather is _____, so we cannot go outside.

3 The _____ uses coal to create electricity.

4 We need a _____ tool as soon as possible.

5 There are too many _____ coming from that car.

6 The _____ car costs more than $30,000.

7 This class _____ students to study very much.

8 You will _____ the water if you pour that liquid into the lake.

9 Each person must pay a _____ to get a driver's license.

10 Coal _____ can be a very dangerous job.

Listening

Now listen to part of a lecture on the topic you just read about.

02-06

Summarizing Read the information below. Use the information to complete the summary for the lecture.

lithium mining	replace a battery	gasoline-powered car
not as good	making EVs	coal-burning power plants

Main Idea The lecturer states that EVs are _____ as people claim they are.

First Supporting Argument The lecturer starts by stating that _____ creates pollution. He then adds that _____ is terrible for the environment and that EVs get recharged with electricity from _____.

Second Supporting Argument Next, the lecturer talks about the prices of EVs. He mentions that they cost around $20,000 more than a _____. In addition, it costs at least $15,000 to _____ on an EV.

Paraphrasing Exercise

Reading The following sentences come from the reading passage summary. Complete each paraphrase with the appropriate words or phrases.

1 The reading passage argues that people have many good reasons to buy electric vehicles.

→ *The reading passage argues that buying electric vehicles provides many _____ for people.*

2 To begin with, the passage explains that electric vehicles are good for the environment.

→ *To begin with, the passage explains that electric vehicles do not _____ the environment.*

3 The reason is that they produce no pollutants.

→ *The reason is that they do not _____ any pollutants.*

4 The passage then argues that electric vehicles do not require much maintenance.

→ *The passage then argues that electric vehicles do not need to be _____ very often.*

5 Unlike internal combustion engines, which often break down, the engines of EVs do not.

→ *Unlike internal combustion engines, which often _____ working, the engines of EVs do not.*

Listening The following sentences come from the lecture summary. Complete each paraphrase with the appropriate words or phrases.

1 The lecturer states that EVs are not as good as people claim they are.

→ *The lecturer comments that EVs are _____ than people say that they are.*

2 The lecturer starts by stating that making EVs creates pollution.

→ *The lecturer begins by stating that _____ EVs makes pollution.*

3 He then adds that lithium mining is terrible for the environment and that EVs get recharged with electricity from coal-burning power plants.

→ *He then adds that lithium mining is terrible for the environment and that EVs _____ electricity from coal-burning power plants.*

4 Next, the lecturer talks about the prices of EVs.

→ *Next, the lecturer talks about how much EVs _____ .*

5 He mentions that they cost around $20,000 more than a gasoline-powered car.

→ *He mentions that they can be around $20,000 more _____ than a gasoline-powered car.*

Tandem Note-Taking

Refer to the summary exercises for the reading and the listening. Paraphrase them to complete the side-by-side notes below. Include only the two points from the reading and the listening that clearly contradict each other.

READING

Main Idea

There are many good reasons to buy

electric vehicles.

First Supporting Argument

Electric vehicles are

Supporting Detail

produce no   ;

batteries

Second Supporting Argument

Electric vehicles do not need

Supporting Detail

engines do not break down; do not need

to

LISTENING

Main Idea

Electric vehicles are not as good as

people claim.

First Supporting Argument

EVs created

Supporting Detail

making EVs creates pollution; lithium

mining   ;

EVs recharged by

Second Supporting Argument

EVs are not

Supporting Detail

$20,000 more than gas-powered cars   ;

$15,000 to

Writing

Use this page to write your response. You have 20 minutes to complete your essay.

Writing Guide	Summarize the points made in the lecture, being sure to explain how they challenge specific arguments made in the reading passage.

First Paragraph ○

State and discuss thesis

_____
_____
_____

Second Paragraph ○

First main idea from lecture

Contradiction from reading

Supporting detail

_____
_____
_____
_____

Third Paragraph ○

Second main idea from lecture

Contradiction from reading

Supporting detail

_____
_____
_____
_____

Fourth Paragraph ○

Conclusion (optional)

_____
_____
_____
_____

✂ **SCAFFOLDING** Here are some useful phrases to help you when you write.

✓ The lecturer talks about…

✓ His arguments go against the ones made…

✓ First, the lecturer mentions that EVs…

✓ However, the lecturer explains that…

✓ Finally, recharging the batteries…

✓ Next, the lecturer claims that…

✓ He points out that…

✓ This argument challenges the claim in…

Read the response carefully to see what makes a response strong.

The lecturer talks about electric vehicles. He believes they are not as good as many people say they are. His arguments go against the ones made in the reading passage.

Firstly, the lecturer mentions that EVs are not really good for the environment. He says that making EVs produces harmful emissions. In addition, the lithium used in their batteries has to be mined. However, lithium mining poisons the land and the water. **1** Finally, recharging the batteries uses electricity made in power plants that burn coal. **2** The lecturer's argument goes against the one made in the reading passage. **3** It states that EVs produce no pollutants and are good for the environment.

Next, the lecturer claims that EVs are much more pricey than gas-powered cars. He points out that the batteries need to be replaced sometimes. This can cost $15,000 or more. This argument challenges the claim in the reading passage that EVs do not require much money. The reason is that they do not need maintenance often and rarely break down.

Critical Analysis Refer to the sample response to complete the tasks below.

1 Which of the following sentences is the thesis statement of the response?
   - Ⓐ He believes they are not as good as many people say they are.
   - Ⓑ Firstly, the lecturer mentions that EVs are not really good for the environment.
   - Ⓒ Next, the lecturer claims that EVs are much more pricey than gas-powered cars.

2 Where should the following sentence be added to improve the response?

It also releases many harmful emissions.
   - Ⓐ **1**
   - Ⓑ **2**
   - Ⓒ **3**

3 Which word in the response means "**expensive**"?

4 List the four connecting phrases the writer of the response uses in the second paragraph.

Improving Schools Is Most Important for Development

? Question

Do you agree or disagree with the following statement? Improving schools is the most important factor for the successful development of a country. Use specific reasons and examples to support your answer.

▌ Background & Brainstorming

Read the following background information to learn more about the topic.

Better Schools Lead to More Development, Social Scientists Argue

By Bill Sutter
June 7

Does a country need better schools to become developed? Many social scientists believe so. They argue that large companies such as Samsung and Microsoft need educated employees. These are the types of companies a nation needs to become wealthier. Researchers also point out that educated people usually make more money. These people can therefore spend more money, which also improves a nation's economy. Their final argument is that educated people are less likely to commit crimes. Statistics show that nations with more educated people have lower crime rates.

But not everyone is convinced that better schools lead to development. One argument is that nations must first develop basic industrial services for its people. Building sewers, roads, and houses does not require a large, educated workforce. Critics also argue that good government policies can lead to economic growth. China is a great example of this. Last, the world's richest nation, the United States, does not have the best schools in the world. So good education may not be necessary for the development of a country after all.

Understanding the Background Use the background information to complete the sentences below.

1   Nations must _____ in order to become developed.

2   The United States is the _____ in the world.

3   _____ that make a nation wealthier require educated employees.

4   A nation can develop _____ without a large, educated workforce.

5   Some people are not convinced that a country needs _____ to develop.

6   Economic growth can also occur because of _____ .

7   A nation that has more educated people usually has _____ .

8   Educated people usually spend _____ , which helps improve a country's economy.

Read the sentences below. Decide whether they agree or disagree with the given statement. Then, circle the sentences that are topic sentences.

- In order for a country to develop, it must improve its schools.

- Nations must first provide their people with basic industrial services.

- Intelligent government policies can also result in economic growth.

- Large companies require workers that are well educated.

- Improving other factors is more important for the development of a nation.

- Places with more educated people have less crime.

Agree

Disagree

Generating Ideas Use the ideas you chose in the Selecting Ideas exercise to fill in the blanks below.

Agree

1 A nation must _____ in order to become developed.

2 Well-_____ are less likely to commit crimes.

3 Large companies need employees that have a(n) _____ .

Disagree

1 _____ must be improved in order for a nation to develop.

2 A nation with good _____ can also grow its economy.

3 People of a nation must have _____ first.

Developing Ideas You have now examined the two options. Which of the two do you feel more comfortable developing into an essay? Explain why you feel this way.

◼ Planning

Do you agree or disagree with the following statement? Improving schools is the most important factor for the successful development of a country. Use specific reasons and examples to support your answer.

Agree

Thesis Statement

I believe that a nation must develop its

schools in order to become developed.

First Supporting Idea

Supporting Example

Second Supporting Idea

Supporting Example

Conclusion

Disagree

Thesis Statement

I feel that other factors must be improved

for a nation to develop.

First Supporting Idea

Supporting Example

Second Supporting Idea

Supporting Example

Conclusion

Writing

Use this page to write your response. You have 30 minutes to complete your essay.

Do you agree or disagree with the following statement? Improving schools is the most important factor for the successful development of a country. Use specific reasons and examples to support your answer.

First Paragraph

State and discuss thesis

_____

_____

_____

Second Paragraph

First main supporting idea

Supporting detail

Example

_____

_____

_____

_____

Third Paragraph

Second main supporting idea

Supporting detail

Example

_____

_____

_____

_____

Fourth Paragraph

Conclusion

_____

_____

_____

_____

SCAFFOLDING Here are some useful phrases to help you when you write.

✓ The most important factor for the development of a country is…

✓ However, I believe that two other factors are…

✓ One important factor for the development of a country is…

✓ Consider the development of…

✓ Additionally, a nation must…

✓ A good example of this is…

✓ Studies show that nations with…

✓ Even so, I firmly believe that…

Sample Response

Read the response carefully to see what makes a response strong.

Many countries around the world are quickly developing these days. Education is certainly an important factor for the successful development of a country. However, I believe that two other factors are more important for a nation's development. These are basic industrial development and good government policies.

One important factor for the development of a nation is the providing of basic industrial services. A nation simply cannot develop without industry. Therefore, a nation must develop its basic industries first. Consider the development of Korea. In the 1960s, Korea quickly developed its industry. The nation constructed roads, sewers, and power plants. This enabled other types of development to occur afterward. Korea developed its industry first. Then, it began focusing on other types of development.

Additionally, a nation must create good government policies to become developed. Good policies allow a country's economy to grow quickly. Some of these policies include trade and money policies. This resulting economic growth can greatly improve people's lives. A good example of this is China. Most people in China are not well educated. Nevertheless, its economy continues to grow. Now, it is one of the richest countries in the world. This is the result of good government policies that have grown China's economy.

Education is necessary for the growth and development of a nation. Even so, I firmly believe that the development of industry and good government policies are more important for a country to become developed.

Critical Analysis Refer to the sample response to complete the tasks below.

1 Which of the following sentences is the thesis statement of the response?

    Ⓐ These are basic industrial development and good government policies.

    Ⓑ However, I believe that two other factors are more important for a nation's development.

    Ⓒ Education is certainly an important factor for the successful development of a country.

2 Which sentence below is closest in meaning to the underlined sentence?

    Ⓐ All development occurs during a time of great industrial development.

    Ⓑ Industrial development must occur first for other development to happen later.

    Ⓒ A nation can develop its industry after it develops other things first.

3 List the two connecting words the writer uses in the third paragraph.

Part B

Chapter 07

Integrated Writing   Astronomy: The Benefits of Space Exploration

Independent Writing   Attending a Live Performance or Watching One on TV

Astronomy: **The Benefits of Space Exploration**

🎯 **Vocabulary** Take a few moments to review the vocabulary items that will appear in this task.

- **exploration** *n.* the act of going to a place that one knows little about
  The team began its **exploration** of the ocean floor.

- **advance** *v.* to move forward
  You will **advance** to the next level after you beat this monster.

- **government** *n.* a system of ruling or controlling
  The president is the head of the **government**.

- **bacteria** *n.* extremely small and simple animals
  There are millions of **bacteria** all over your body.

- **volcano** *n.* an opening in the ground where very hot rocks come out
  The Hawaiian Islands have many **volcanoes**.

- **astound** *v.* to impress strongly by doing something unexpected; to amaze
  I am **astounded** that you solved the puzzle so quickly.

- **poverty** *n.* the state of being poor; not having money
  Many people in Africa live in **poverty**.

- **affect** *v.* to create a change in something
  The medicine did not **affect** my cold.

- **address** *v.* to concentrate on; to focus on
  We need to **address** this problem immediately.

- **donate** *v.* to give something as a gift
  My parents have **donated** thousands of dollars to cancer research.

Words and Expressions Refer to the vocabulary to fill in the blanks below. You may need to change the forms of the words.

1 To kill _____ on your food, you must cook it properly.

2 Almost every nation in the world is controlled by a(n) _____.

3 Any changes you make at the top _____ the layout at the bottom.

4 The group members _____ their time to help homeless people.

5 Cave _____ is fun, but it can be dangerous.

6 Our manager _____ the project in her speech today.

7 That _____ has not erupted in over 100 years.

8 Unfortunately, not every student was able to _____ to the next grade.

9 Giving people good jobs helps get them out of _____.

10 His ability to play the piano _____ the audience.

Reading

Read the passage carefully. Try to understand what the main argument of the passage is. You have 3 minutes to read.

Each year, the United States and the European Union spend billions of dollars on space exploration. They argue that space exploration helps advance the human race. While space exploration has some benefits, governments should keep their focus on the Earth.

For one, much of the Earth still has not been explored. Around ninety-five percent of the oceans have not been explored. Scientists therefore continue to make new discoveries there all the time. For instance, ocean researchers recently found a new type of bacteria. The bacteria live deep in the ocean. They are special because they get energy from volcanoes on the ocean floor. This finding astounded scientists. It showed them that they still have many things left to discover on our own planet.

Perhaps more important is the fact that there are still many problems on the Earth. Problems such as war, poverty, and hunger affect billions of people across the globe. Instead of exploring space, governments need to address these problems first. For example, several governments spend billions of dollars on the International Space Station each year. These governments could instead donate that money. The money could help thousands of poor people improve their lives. On the whole, governments need to fix the problems here on the Earth before going into outer space.

Summarizing Read the information below. Use the information to complete the summary for the reading passage.

been explored	many problems	International Space Station
focus on the Earth	new discoveries	donate the money

Main Idea The writer believes that governments should _____ rather than spend money on space exploration.

First Supporting Argument First, much of the Earth still has not _____ . The text then states that scientists continue to make _____ all the time.

Second Supporting Argument There are still _____ on the Earth that need to be solved. Instead of spending money on the _____ , governments should _____ to those in need.

⊙ Vocabulary Take a few moments to review the vocabulary items that will appear in this task.

- **bring about** *phr v.* to make something happen
  We can **bring about** real change if we work together.

- **development** *n.* an improvement; growth
  We allow young people to reach their dreams by assisting them in their personal **development**.

- **key** *adj.* most important; significant
  The **key** factor to remember is to keep your head above water.

- **colonization** *n.* the act of making a home in a new place
  Britain began its **colonization** of Australia in the eighteenth century.

- **crowded** *adj.* filled as much as possible; cramped
  The bus is too **crowded** for me to sit.

- **the human race** *n.* all human beings
  We are all members of **the human race**.

- **exist** *v.* to live; to be real
  Ghosts do not **exist**, so you do not need to be afraid of them.

- **modern** *adj.* of current times; present
  I like classical music more than **modern** music.

Words and Expressions Refer to the vocabulary to fill in the blanks below. You may need to change the forms of the words.

1 This coffee shop is too _____. I want to go somewhere quieter.

2 My neighborhood is currently experiencing many major _____.

3 In the future, _____ will take place in outer space.

4 I like her clothing designs because they are so _____.

5 This recipe's _____ ingredients are salt and pepper.

6 We were going to visit the park, but it no longer _____.

7 _____ cannot survive without cooperation.

8 Modern technology has _____ many changes in our lives.

Listening

Now listen to part of a lecture on the topic you just read about.

02-07

Summarizing Read the information below. Use the information to complete the summary for the lecture.

colonization	building colonies	modern personal computer
human body	scientific advancements	continue our exploration

Main Idea The instructor presents two reasons why we must _____ of outer space.

First Supporting Argument The opening argument deals with _____. The Earth will become very crowded in the future. By traveling into space, we can learn how space affects the _____ in the long term. We can also start _____ in space.

Second Supporting Argument There are also the _____ that have come from space exploration. Space exploration led to the development of the _____.

Paraphrasing Exercise

Reading The following sentences come from the reading passage summary. Complete each paraphrase with the appropriate words or phrases.

1 The writer believes that governments should focus on the Earth rather than spend money on space exploration.

→ *The author of the passage feels that governments should _____ on the Earth instead of spending money on exploring space.*

2 First, much of the Earth still has not been explored.

→ *To begin with, there are still many things on the Earth to _____.*

3 For this reason, scientists still make new discoveries all the time.

→ *Consequently, researchers _____ to make new discoveries.*

4 There are still many problems that need to be solved on the Earth.

→ *Additionally, the Earth has several problems that must be _____.*

5 Instead of spending money on the International Space Station, governments should donate the money to those in need.

→ *Governments should _____ to needy people rather than spend it on space research.*

Listening The following sentences come from the lecture summary. Complete each paraphrase with the appropriate words or phrases.

1 The instructor presents two reasons why we must continue our exploration of outer space.

→ *In the lecture, the instructor gives two arguments in favor of _____.*

2 The Earth will become very crowded in the future.

→ *The Earth will eventually become _____.*

3 By traveling into space, we can learn how space affects the human body in the long term.

→ *Traveling into space _____ us how outer space causes changes in the human body.*

4 There are also the scientific advancements that have come from space exploration.

→ *Several scientific _____ have occurred because of space exploration.*

5 Space exploration led to the development of the modern personal computer.

→ *Space exploration led to the _____ of the present personal computers.*

Tandem Note-Taking

Refer to the summary exercises for the reading and the listening. Paraphrase them to complete the side-by-side notes below. Include only the two points from the reading and the listening that clearly contradict each other.

READING

Main Idea

The author of the passage feels that governments should concentrate on the Earth.

First Supporting Argument

There are still many things on the Earth to

Supporting Detail

recently discovered

Second Supporting Argument

The Earth has several problems

Supporting Detail

governments should

LISTENING

Main Idea

The speaker feels that we must continue our exploration of space.

First Supporting Argument

The Earth will eventually become

Supporting Detail

learn how space causes changes

start building

Second Supporting Argument

Space exploration has led to

Supporting Detail

development of

Writing

Use this page to write your response. You have 20 minutes to complete your essay.

Writing Guide — Summarize the points made in the lecture, being sure to explain how they cast doubt on specific points made in the reading passage.

First Paragraph ○

State and discuss thesis

_____

_____

_____

Second Paragraph ○

First main idea from reading

Contradiction from lecture

Supporting detail

_____

_____

_____

_____

_____

Third Paragraph ○

Second main idea from reading

Contradiction from lecture

Supporting detail

_____

_____

_____

_____

_____

Fourth Paragraph ○

Conclusion (optional)

_____

_____

_____

_____

✂ **SCAFFOLDING** Here are some useful phrases to help you when you write.

✓ The reading passage and the lecture present…

✓ The author of the passage argues…

✓ The instructor, on the other hand, believes…

✓ For her first argument, the instructor talks about…

✓ This argument calls into question the one given in…

✓ The text stated that…

✓ The instructor's second argument deals with…

✓ In the reading passage, however, it is argued…

◗ Sample Response

Read the response carefully to see what makes a response strong.

The topic of the reading passage and the lecture is space exploration. The author of the passage feels that governments should concentrate on the Earth. Yet the instructor feels that we must continue our exploration of space.

First, the reading states that many places on the Earth still have not been explored. In fact, scientists recently discovered bacteria that get energy from volcanoes. On the contrary, the instructor states that the Earth will eventually become overpopulated. The instructor goes on to argue that we must continue to explore space to learn how it causes changes in the human body. We can also start building colonies there.

Next, the passage argues that the Earth has several problems that must be fixed. The author feels that governments should donate money to the needy instead of spending it on space programs. In contrast, the instructor says that space exploration has led to many scientific developments. One of these is the development of the modern personal computer.

Critical Analysis Refer to the sample response to complete the tasks below.

1   Which of the following sentences is the topic sentence of the second paragraph?
   - Ⓐ In fact, scientists recently discovered bacteria that get energy from volcanoes.
   - Ⓑ On the contrary, the instructor states that the Earth will eventually become overpopulated.
   - Ⓒ First, the reading states that many places on the Earth still have not been explored.

2   Which sentence below is closest in meaning to the underlined sentence?
   - Ⓐ According to the writer, governments should give money to the poor instead of spending it on space exploration.
   - Ⓑ The writer believes that governments need to spend more money on their space programs.
   - Ⓒ The author feels that donating money to the needy can help more people than spending money on space programs.

3   Which word in the response means "**present**"?

4   List the three connecting phrases the writer of the response uses in the second paragraph.

Attending a Live Performance or Watching One on TV

Would you prefer to attend a live performance in person, or would you prefer to watch an event on television? Support your answer with specific details.

Background & Brainstorming

Read the following background information to learn more about the topic.

Opinions Divided on Attending Concerts

IDC Business Consulting Services

According to our latest survey, nearly half of all people prefer to attend live performances in person. One reason many people gave is that live performances are more exciting. People want to see the performers up close. Many also said that seeing a performance with a crowd makes the experience more powerful. They want to be with other fans at live performances. Other respondents felt that going to live performances creates special memories. By going to shows with their friends, they will always remember those experiences.

About the same number of people claimed to enjoy watching performances at home. Many people like the fact that staying at home is much cheaper. These people do not want to spend their money on tickets and transportation to see performances live. Several people also feel that seeing performances on television is less time consuming. They do not want to spend extra time traveling to the concert and returning home. Additionally, many like the fact that seeing performances on television is more comfortable. They can watch the performances from anywhere they want.

Understanding the Background Use the background information to complete the sentences below.

1   Many people feel that going to live performances is more _____ .

2   Seeing a performance with a crowd is a(n) _____ for many people.

3   To watch a performance live, you must spend money on _____ .

4   Attending a performance in person creates a(n) _____ .

5   It is less _____ to watch a performance on television.

6   At a live performance, you can see the performer _____ .

7   Watching a performance on television is _____ .

8   You are with _____ at a live performance.

Selecting Ideas Read the phrases below. Decide whether they are about attending a live performance in person or watching it on television. Then, circle the sentences that are topic sentences.

- Watching a performance on television takes much less time than going in person.

- It is better to watch a performance on television.

- You can create a long-lasting memory by going to a live performance.

- Being at a performance in person is superior to watching it on television.

- Attending a live performance is a more powerful experience than seeing it on television.

- Seeing a performance on television is less expensive.

Attend in Person

Watch on Television

Generating Ideas Use the ideas you chose in the Selecting Ideas exercise to fill in the blanks below.

Attend in Person

1 It is _____ to be at a performance in person than to watch it on television.

2 Being at a live show is _____ than seeing it on television.

3 Attending a live performance can create a(n) _____ .

Watch on Television

1 Seeing a performance _____ is better than watching it in person.

2 Watching a performance on television is _____ .

3 Going to a performance takes _____ .

Developing Ideas You have now examined the two options. Which of the two do you feel more comfortable developing into an essay? Explain why you feel this way.

| Planning

Would you prefer to attend a live performance in person, or would you prefer to watch the event on television? Support your answer with specific details.

Attend in Person

Thesis Statement

I would much rather attend a live performance in person.

First Supporting Idea

Supporting Example

Second Supporting Idea

Supporting Example

Conclusion

Watch on Television

Thesis Statement

I prefer watching a performance on television.

First Supporting Idea

Supporting Example

Second Supporting Idea

Supporting Example

Conclusion

Writing

Use this page to write your response. You have 30 minutes to complete your essay.

Writing Guide

Would you prefer to attend a live performance in person, or would you prefer to watch the event on television? Support your answer with specific details.

First Paragraph ○

State and discuss thesis

_____

_____

_____

Second Paragraph ○

First main supporting idea

Supporting detail

Example

_____

_____

_____

_____

Third Paragraph ○

Second main supporting idea

Supporting detail

Example

_____

_____

_____

_____

Fourth Paragraph ○

Conclusion

_____

_____

_____

_____

✂ SCAFFOLDING Here are some useful phrases to help you when you write.

✓ Attending a live performance can be…

✓ Nevertheless, I prefer watching a performance…

✓ To begin with, watching a live performance…

✓ To go into more detail…

✓ In addition, going to a live performance…

✓ On top of this, you have to…

✓ This is especially nice because…

✓ While some people would rather ~, I believe…

Read the response carefully to see what makes a response strong.

Attending a live performance in person can be an exciting and memorable event. Nevertheless, I prefer watching a performance on television because it is less expensive and less time consuming.

To begin with, watching a live performance on television is less expensive than seeing it in person. Tickets to most shows are very costly. To go into more detail, I once went to one of my favorite band's concerts. The tickets cost nearly one hundred dollars per person. The performance was far away, so I had to spend money on transportation. I also bought drinks and dinner. In total, the concert cost me two hundred dollars. Although going to the live performance was a lot of fun, I felt that it was just too expensive.

Going to a live performance takes a lot of time, too. A performance by itself usually lasts a few hours. On top of this, you have to travel to the concert and back home again. This alone can sometimes take several hours. Compare this with watching a performance on television. You only spend time watching the performance. You do not have to waste time going to and then leaving the performance. This is especially beneficial because most performances end very late at night. In short, watching a live performance on television is much better because it saves time.

While some people would rather see a live performance in person, I believe watching it on television is better because it is cheaper and saves a lot of time.

Critical Analysis Refer to the sample response to complete the tasks below.

1 Which of the following sentences is the thesis statement of the response?

   (A) While some people would rather see a live performance in person, I believe watching it on television is better because it is cheaper and saves a lot of time.

   (B) Nevertheless, I prefer watching a performance on television because it is less expensive and less time consuming.

   (C) Attending a live performance in person can be an exciting and memorable event.

2 Which of the following sentences gives an example for the second paragraph?

   (A) The tickets cost nearly one hundred dollars per person.

   (B) Tickets to most shows are very costly.

   (C) To begin with, watching a live performance on television is less expensive than seeing it in person.

3 List the two connecting phrases the writer uses in the third paragraph.

Part B

Chapter 08

Ecology: **Using Solar Energy Rather than Fossil Fuels**

🎯 **Vocabulary** Take a few moments to review the vocabulary items that will appear in this task.

- **traditional energy source** *n.* coal, oil, or gas
  Traditional energy sources are not good for the environment.

- **alternative energy source** *n.* energy that comes from the sun, wind, or water
  Alternative energy sources are becoming more popular today.

- **solution** *n.* the answer to a problem
  The solution to two plus two is four.

- **poison** *n.* something that causes illness or death
  We used poison to kill the rats in our house.

- **gas** *n.* something not solid or liquid
  The air we breathe is a gas.

- **pollution** *n.* something that harms living things and dirties the environment
  Cars are a major source of pollution today.

- **panel** *n.* a flat, rectangular piece of material
  My front door has four panels on it.

- **constantly** *adv.* without stopping; continually
  She constantly complained about her job.

- **forever** *adv.* for a limitless time; endlessly
  No one can live forever.

Words and Expressions Refer to the vocabulary to fill in the blanks below. You may need to change the forms of the words.

1   New energy technology has reduced _____ levels around the world.

2   Most cars still run on _____ such as gasoline.

3   The weather in this area changes _____ from hot to cold.

4   What is your _____ to the housing problem?

5   Consuming even a small amount of _____ can make you very sick.

6   The company wants to use _____ to keep the environment clean.

7   Reading this book changed my life _____ .

8   The control _____ of the machine has many buttons on it.

9   Carbon dioxide is a(n) _____ made up of one part carbon and two parts oxygen.

Reading

Read the passage carefully. Try to understand what the main argument of the passage is. You have 3 minutes to read.

Modern society relies on traditional sources of energy such as coal and gasoline. The problem with this is that these energy sources cause great harm to the planet. Therefore, we must use alternative energy sources. Of these alternative sources, solar energy offers the greatest advantages.

One important benefit of solar energy is that it is environmentally friendly. Traditional energy sources release poison gases into the air. This is a major source of pollution. Solar energy, in contrast, does not cause pollution. It is clean because it relies only on the power of the sun. Solar energy works by using special panels that collect the sun's energy. These panels turn the sun's energy into usable electricity. This happens without polluting the environment.

Low cost is another advantage of solar energy. Making energy from coal and fossil fuels can be expensive. Energy companies have to search for coal and oil constantly. This costs a lot of time and money. Solar energy is different. It only requires only two things. The first is the sun's energy. This is available for free almost everywhere. The second is solar panels. Once these panels are installed, it is possible to use the sun's energy forever at no cost.

Summarizing Read the information below. Use the information to complete the summary for the reading passage.

special panels	environmentally friendly	low cost
sun's energy	causing pollution	perfect solution
at no cost		

Main Idea The reading says that solar energy is the _____ for the world's energy problems.

First Supporting Argument The first benefit of solar energy is that it is _____ Solar energy works by using _____ to collect the sun's energy. This happens without _____.

Second Supporting Argument An additional advantage of solar energy is its _____. Solar energy uses the _____ and solar panels. These make it possible to use the sun's energy forever _____.

🎯 Vocabulary Take a few moments to review the vocabulary items that will appear in this task.

- **drawback** *n.* a condition that makes something difficult; a disadvantage

  Owning a house has both benefits and **drawbacks**.

- **replace** *v.* to take the place of something or someone

  Harold **replaced** Sylvia as the leader of the group.

- **average** *adj.* common; normal

  The **average** family has two children.

- **efficient** *adj.* productive without waste

  Hybrid cars are more **efficient** than traditional cars.

- **supplement** *v.* to add to something to improve or complete it

  I will **supplement** your textbook with this news article.

- **hidden cost** *n.* a disadvantage that is not known right away

  Many products that are said to be safe for the environment have several **hidden costs**.

- **afford** *v.* to have enough money to pay for something

  My family cannot **afford** to go on vacation this year.

- **maintenance** *n.* the act of keeping something in good condition; repair

  In order to keep your computer working properly, you must often perform **maintenance** on it.

- **fee** *n.* a charge made for something done; a payment

  The doctor's **fees** are much too expensive.

- **sensitive** *adj.* easily hurt or damaged

  Try not to make Melissa upset. You know she is a **sensitive** person.

Words and Expressions Refer to the vocabulary to fill in the blanks below. You may need to change the forms of the words.

1 I suggest you _____ your diet by taking these vitamins.

2 How can you _____ to buy so many things for your home?

3 I take my car to the mechanic for _____ every three months.

4 We had to _____ our television because the old one did not work well.

5 You have to pay an extra _____ to make video calls.

6 In this country, the _____ worker makes $25,000 a year.

7 The _____ of learning a foreign language is losing some of your first language skills.

8 A perfectly _____ machine makes the same amount of energy it uses.

9 This film is very _____. Be sure not to take it out in the light.

10 The high cost of a college education is its main _____.

Listening

Now listen to part of a lecture on the topic you just read about.

02-08

Summarizing Read the information below. Use the information to complete the summary for the lecture.

less efficient	maintenance fees	the drawbacks
traditional energy sources	to afford	hidden cost

Main Idea The lecturer outlines some of _____ of solar energy. The lecturer supports his opinion with two examples.

First Supporting Argument For his first argument, the lecturer states that solar energy cannot replace _____. The reason is that solar panels are _____ than energy sources such as coal.

Second Supporting Argument The next reason the lecturer mentions is the _____ of solar energy. He explains that solar energy panels are too expensive for most people _____. He also says that they have high _____ .

Paraphrasing Exercise

Reading The following sentences come from the reading passage summary. Complete each paraphrase with the appropriate words or phrases.

1 The reading claims that solar energy is the perfect solution for our energy problems.

→ *The passage claims that the* _____ *to our energy problems is solar power.*

2 The first benefit of solar energy is that it is environmentally friendly.

→ *One advantage of solar energy is that it is* _____ .

3 Solar energy works by using special panels to collect the sun's energy.

→ *Solar energy uses special panels to* _____ *the sun's energy.*

4 An additional advantage of solar energy is its low cost.

→ *Another benefit of solar energy is that it is* _____ .

5 These panels make it possible to use the sun's energy forever at no cost.

→ *The panels allow us to use solar energy* _____ *free of charge.*

Listening The following sentences come from the lecture summary. Complete each paraphrase with the appropriate words or phrases.

1 The lecturer outlines some of the drawbacks of solar energy.

→ *The lecturer talks about some of the* _____ *of solar energy.*

2 For his first argument, the lecturer states that solar energy cannot replace traditional energy sources.

→ *The first argument given by the lecturer is that solar energy cannot* _____ *traditional sources of energy.*

3 The next reason the lecturer mentions is the hidden cost of solar energy.

→ *The lecturer also* _____ *that solar energy has hidden costs.*

4 He explains that solar energy panels are too expensive for most people to afford.

→ *He states that few people are able* _____ *solar energy panels.*

5 He also says that they have high maintenance fees.

→ *The lecturer also mentions that the panels have high* _____ .

Tandem Note-Taking

Refer to the summary exercises for the reading and the listening. Paraphrase them to complete the side-by-side notes below. Include only the two points from the reading and the listening that clearly contradict each other.

READING

Main Idea

The passage claims that the best answer

to our energy problems is solar power.

First Supporting Argument

One advantage of solar energy is that

Supporting Detail

uses special panels to

; does not cause

Second Supporting Argument

Another benefit of solar energy is

Supporting Detail

able to use solar energy

LISTENING

Main Idea

The instructor talks about some of the

disadvantages of solar energy.

First Supporting Argument

Solar energy cannot

Supporting Detail

solar panels are less

Second Supporting Argument

Solar energy has

Supporting Detail

few people able

; have high

| Writing

Use this page to write your response. You have 20 minutes to complete your essay.

Writing Guide	Summarize the points made in the lecture, being sure to explain how they challenge specific claims made in the reading passage.

First Paragraph ○

State and discuss thesis

_____
_____
_____

Second Paragraph ○

First main idea from lecture

Contradiction from reading

Supporting detail

_____
_____
_____
_____
_____

Third Paragraph ○

Second main idea from lecture

Contradiction from reading

Supporting detail

_____
_____
_____
_____
_____

Fourth Paragraph ○

Conclusion (optional)

_____
_____
_____
_____

✂ **SCAFFOLDING** Here are some useful phrases to help you when you write.

✓ The reading passage and the lecture both deal with…

✓ The passage claims that…

✓ The lecturer talks about…

✓ The opening argument of the lecture is…

✓ To explain why, the lecturer mentions…

✓ At the same time, the reading claims…

✓ The lecturer's next argument is…

✓ However, the lecturer shows…

Read the response carefully to see what makes a response strong.

The reading passage and the lecture both deal with the issue of solar energy. The passage states that the best answer to our energy problems is solar power. In contrast, the lecturer talks about the disadvantages of solar energy.

The opening argument of the lecture is that solar energy cannot take the place of traditional energy sources. To explain why, the lecturer mentions that solar panels are much less efficient than traditional energy sources such as coal. Because of this, solar energy can only supplement traditional sources of energy. At the same time, the reading argues that solar energy must replace other energy sources. The reason is that solar energy is good for the environment.

The lecturer's next argument is that solar energy has hidden costs. The reading passage states that solar energy is not expensive because the sun's energy is free. **❶** However, the lecturer explains that solar energy has hidden costs. He says that one solar panel costs more than ten thousand dollars. **❷** He also explains that solar panels have high repair costs. **❸**

Critical Analysis Refer to the sample response to complete the tasks below.

1   Which of the following sentences is the opening sentence of the response?

    Ⓐ   The lecturer talks about some of the disadvantages of solar energy.

    Ⓑ   The passage claims that the best answer to our energy problems is solar power.

    Ⓒ   The reading passage and the lecture both deal with the issue of solar energy.

2   Where should the following sentence be added to improve the response?

    This means that few people can afford to buy solar panels.

    Ⓐ   ❶

    Ⓑ   ❷

    Ⓒ   ❸

3   Which word in the response means "**to add to something**"?

4   List the three connecting phrases the writer of the response uses in the second paragraph.

It Is Better to Save Money than to Spend It

Question

Do you agree or disagree with the following statement? It is better to save money than to spend it. Use specific reasons and example to support your answer.

Background & Brainstorming

Read the following background information to learn more about the topic.

Business Review Monthly: Reader Letters

Thank you for last week's money article. It was great to learn the benefits of spending money. I realized that spending just a little money can make my life better now. That is why I bought a new television for my house. I will also spend money to make other people happy. I know my family will be much happier if I take them on vacation instead of putting money in a savings account. Plus, you never know what will happen in the future. I may win the lottery and not need to save money for retirement.

Daniel Harrison
San Francisco, California

I believe the author of the money article gave people bad advice. People need to save more money, not spend it. For one, saving money now allows you to have more money later. Money put in a savings account earns interest and increases in value. Similarly, saving money allows you to make larger purchases later. You can buy a nicer car or a bigger house if you save. Last, but not least, saving a lot of money lets you retire sooner. Then, you can enjoy your life more when you are older.

C.P. Barker
Michigan

Understanding the Background Use the background information to complete the sentences below.

1   Saving money now allows you to have _____ later.

2   Spending just _____ will make you happier now.

3   The money in a savings account will earn interest and _____ .

4   It is possible to buy a nice car or a(n) _____ if you save your money.

5   You can spend money to make other people _____ .

6   Saving money also allows you to _____ when you are not that old.

7   You should also spend money because you never know _____ in the future.

8   Taking your family _____ will make them happier than putting money in a savings account.

Selecting Ideas Read the sentences below. Decide whether they agree or disagree with the given statement. Then, circle the sentences that are topic sentences.

- Spending money can make other people happy.

- You can make large purchases that improve your life by saving money.

- Spending money is preferable to saving money.

- It is important to save as much money as possible.

- It is not possible to know the future, so it is better to spend your money.

- Saving money is necessary to retire at a younger age.

Agree

Disagree

Generating Ideas Use the ideas you chose in the Selecting Ideas exercise to fill in the blanks below.

Agree

1 You should save as _____ as possible.

2 Making _____ can make your life better.

3 To finish working sooner, you must _____.

Disagree

1 It is better to _____ than to save it.

2 Other people can be _____ if you spend money.

3 You do not know what will happen _____.

Developing Ideas You have now examined the two options. Which of the two do you feel more comfortable developing into an essay? Explain why you feel this way.

Planning

Do you agree or disagree with the following statement? It is better to save money than to spend it. Use specific reasons and examples to support your answer.

Agree

Thesis Statement

I feel that saving money is preferable to spending it.

First Supporting Idea

Supporting Example

Second Supporting Idea

Supporting Example

Conclusion

Disagree

Thesis Statement

I believe that it is better to spend money than to save it.

First Supporting Idea

Supporting Example

Second Supporting Idea

Supporting Example

Conclusion

Writing

Use this page to write your response. You have 30 minutes to complete your essay.

Writing Guide

Do you agree or disagree with the following statement? It is better to save money than to spend it. Use specific reasons and examples to support your answer.

First Paragraph ◉

State and discuss thesis

_____
_____
_____
_____

Second Paragraph ◉

First main supporting idea

Supporting detail

Example

_____
_____
_____
_____
_____
_____

Third Paragraph ◉

Second main supporting idea

Supporting detail

Example

_____
_____
_____
_____
_____
_____

Fourth Paragraph ◉

Conclusion

_____
_____
_____
_____

⚒ SCAFFOLDING Here are some useful phrases to help you when you write.

✓ I agree that ~ is better than…

✓ The first reason is that…

✓ First of all, saving money allows you to…

✓ By spending money, you can…

✓ Another advantage of saving money is…

✓ For instance, my mother's parents…

✓ This taught me that spending money…

✓ Ultimately, I strongly believe that…

Read the response carefully to see what makes a response strong.

I agree that saving money is better than spending it. The first reason is that saving money allows you to improve your life. The second reason is that you can retire sooner.

First of all, saving money allows you to improve your life. You can easily make large purchases that make your life better. For example, my dad saved money for many years when he was younger. After saving for about ten years, he had enough money to buy a large house. Now, my father does not have to waste money paying rent. At the same time, we live a very nice life. Saving money allows you to improve your overall quality of life.

Another advantage of saving money is that it allows you to retire sooner. If you do not save a lot of money, then you will have to work until you are very old. For instance, my mother's parents did not save much money and had to work their entire lives. My father's parents were much different. They started saving when they were young. By the time they were fifty, they had enough money to retire and to live very comfortable lives. This taught me that by saving money, you can make sure that your life is comfortable when you are older.

Ultimately, I strongly believe that saving money is much better than spending it. Having money allows you to live a better life and lets you retire sooner.

Critical Analysis Refer to the sample response to complete the tasks below.

1 Which of the following sentences is the topic sentence of the third paragraph?

Ⓐ This taught me that by saving money, you can make sure that your life is comfortable when you are older.

Ⓑ For instance, my mother's parents did not save much money and had to work their entire lives.

Ⓒ Another advantage of saving money is that it allows you to retire sooner.

2 Which of the following sentences is the final comment of the response?

Ⓐ Ultimately, I strongly believe that saving money is much better than spending it.

Ⓑ I agree that saving money is better than spending it.

Ⓒ Having money allows you to live a better life and lets you retire sooner.

3 List the three connecting phrases the writer uses in the second paragraph.

Part C

Experiencing the TOEFL iBT Actual Tests

CONTINUE   VOLUME

Writing Section Directions

03-01

 Make sure your headset is on.

This section measures your ability to use writing to communicate in an academic environment. There will be two writing tasks.

For the first writing task, you will read a passage and listen to a lecture and then answer a question based on what you have read and heard. For the second writing task, you will answer a question based on your own knowledge and experience.

Now listen to the directions for the first writing task.

Writing Based on Reading and Listening

03-02

For this task, you will first have **3 minutes** to read a passage about an academic topic. You may take notes on the passage if you wish. The passage will then be removed and you will listen to a lecture about the same topic. While you listen, you may also take notes.

Then you will have **20 minutes** to write a response to a question that asks you about the relationship between the lecture you heard and the reading passage. Try to answer the question as completely as possible using information from the reading passage and the lecture. The question does **not** ask you to express your personal opinion. You will be able to see the reading passage again when it is time for you to write. You may use your notes to help you answer the question.

Typically, an effective response will be 150 to 225 words long. Your response will be judged on the quality of your writing and on the completeness and accuracy of the content. If you finish your response before time is up, you may click on **Next** to go on to the second writing task.

Now you will see the reading passage for 3 minutes. Remember it will be available to you again while you are writing. Immediately after the reading time ends, the lecture will begin, so keep your headset on until the lecture is over.

At times, people observe fish leaping out of the water. Scientists have studied this behavior and have developed theories on why fish act this way.

First, some fish leap out of the water to avoid predators. Many fish are carnivores. So they hunt and eat other fish. Sudden attacks are often their preferred hunting method. When a smaller fish detects a bigger one attacking it, it attempts to escape. In some cases, such as when the attack comes from below, the smaller fish flees by moving upward. This results in the fish leaping from the water as it tries to get away.

Additionally, some fish live in environments with low oxygen levels. This is especially common in ponds and lakes. At times, algae grow out of control and remove the oxygen from the water. In these instances, fish leap out of the water to attempt to get oxygen. There are some fish that have evolved to be able to breathe air. These include the snakehead and the African sharp-toothed catfish. These fish—and other ones similar to them—are simply trying to stay alive by getting oxygen.

03-03

Directions You have 20 minutes to plan and write your response. Your response will be judged on the basis of the quality of your writing and on how well your response presents the points in the lecture and their relationship to the reading passage. Typically, an effective response will be 150 to 225 words.

Question Summarize the main points in the lecture, being sure to explain how they challenge specific claims made in the reading passage.

At times, people observe fish leaping out of the water. Scientists have studied this behavior and have developed theories on why fish act this way.

First, some fish leap out of the water to avoid predators. Many fish are carnivores. So they hunt and eat other fish. Sudden attacks are often their preferred hunting method. When a smaller fish detects a bigger one attacking it, it attempts to escape. In some cases, such as when the attack comes from below, the smaller fish flees by moving upward. This results in the fish leaping from the water as it tries to get away.

Additionally, some fish live in environments with low oxygen levels. This is especially common in ponds and lakes. At times, algae grow out of control and remove the oxygen from the water. In these instances, fish leap out of the water to attempt to get oxygen. There are some fish that have evolved to be able to breathe air. These include the snakehead and the African sharp-toothed catfish. These fish— and other ones similar to them—are simply trying to stay alive by getting oxygen.

Task 2

Writing Based on Knowledge and Experience

03-04

For this task, you will write an essay in response to a question that asks you to state, explain, and support your opinion on an issue. You will have **30 minutes** to write your essay.

Typically, an effective essay will contain a minimum of 300 words. Your essay will be judged on the quality of your writing. This includes the development of your ideas, the organization of your essay, and the quality and accuracy of the language you use to express ideas.

Click on **Continue** to go on.

Directions Read the question below. You have 30 minutes to plan, write, and revise your essay. Typically, an effective response will contain a minimum of 300 words.

Question

Do you agree or disagree with the following statement?

People should not have to pay to use public transportation.

Use specific reasons and examples to support your answer.

CONTINUE   VOLUME

03-05

Writing Section Directions

 Make sure your headset is on.

This section measures your ability to use writing to communicate in an academic environment. There will be two writing tasks.

For the first writing task, you will read a passage and listen to a lecture and then answer a question based on what you have read and heard. For the second writing task, you will answer a question based on your own knowledge and experience.

Now listen to the directions for the first writing task.

Task 1

Writing Based on Reading and Listening

03-06

For this task, you will first have **3 minutes** to read a passage about an academic topic. You may take notes on the passage if you wish. The passage will then be removed and you will listen to a lecture about the same topic. While you listen, you may also take notes.

Then you will have **20 minutes** to write a response to a question that asks you about the relationship between the lecture you heard and the reading passage. Try to answer the question as completely as possible using information from the reading passage and the lecture. The question does **not** ask you to express your personal opinion. You will be able to see the reading passage again when it is time for you to write. You may use your notes to help you answer the question.

Typically, an effective response will be 150 to 225 words long. Your response will be judged on the quality of your writing and on the completeness and accuracy of the content. If you finish your response before time is up, you may click on **Next** to go on to the second writing task.

Now you will see the reading passage for 3 minutes. Remember it will be available to you again while you are writing. Immediately after the reading time ends, the lecture will begin, so keep your headset on until the lecture is over.

As companies become more successful, their leaders often consider expanding. They believe they will profit by becoming larger for a couple of reasons.

One reason is that as bigger companies, they will have less competition. There are a large number of small companies. But there are much fewer big ones. As a general rule, small companies compete with small ones. And big companies compete with big ones. By increasing a company's size, its leaders can make it more competitive. In many cases, bigger companies enjoy more success. Their revenues increase. And their profits also become larger as they grow in size.

In addition, bigger companies can produce more products. Small companies are limited in the number of products they can make and sell. For instance, a small car manufacturer may only make a few hundred cars each year. And they will all be the same model. However, a larger car maker can make thousands of cars annually. They will also be from different models. As a result, the larger car marker can sell a greater number of vehicles. Then, it will profit much more than the small company.

03-07

Directions You have 20 minutes to plan and write your response. Your response will be judged on the basis of the quality of your writing and on how well your response presents the points in the lecture and their relationship to the reading passage. Typically, an effective response will be 150 to 225 words.

Question Summarize the main points in the lecture, being sure to explain how they challenge specific claims made in the reading passage.

As companies become more successful, their leaders often consider expanding. They believe they will profit by becoming larger for a couple of reasons.

One reason is that as bigger companies, they will have less competition. There are a large number of small companies. But there are much fewer big ones. As a general rule, small companies compete with small ones. And big companies compete with big ones. By increasing a company's size, its leaders can make it more competitive. In many cases, bigger companies enjoy more success. Their revenues increase. And their profits also become larger as they grow in size.

In addition, bigger companies can produce more products. Small companies are limited in the number of products they can make and sell. For instance, a small car manufacturer may only make a few hundred cars each year. And they will all be the same model. However, a larger car maker can make thousands of cars annually. They will also be from different models. As a result, the larger car marker can sell a greater number of vehicles. Then, it will profit much more than the small company.

Writing Based on
Knowledge and Experience

03-08

For this task, you will write an essay in response to a question that asks you to state, explain, and support your opinion on an issue. You will have **30 minutes** to write your essay.

Typically, an effective essay will contain a minimum of 300 words. Your essay will be judged on the quality of your writing. This includes the development of your ideas, the organization of your essay, and the quality and accuracy of the language you use to express ideas.

Click on **Continue** to go on.

Directions Read the question below. You have 30 minutes to plan, write, and revise your essay. Typically, an effective response will contain a minimum of 300 words.

Question

Do you agree or disagree with the following statement?

Schools need to teach students basic economic skills.

Use specific reasons and examples to support your answer.

Appendix

MASTER WORD LIST

⭐ MASTER WORD LIST

Chapter 1

- **bank teller** *n.* a person who works at a bank and gives and receives money

  When young, my younger sister worked as a **bank teller** in Boston.

- **communicate** *v.* to exchange ideas by writing or speech

  The soap opera is about two neighbors who can't **communicate** with each other.

- **concentrate** *v.* to think about; to focus on

  He decided to **concentrate** all his efforts on his writing.

- **conduct** *v.* to lead; to do

  Mr. Jenkins will **conduct** a tour of the museum.

- **develop** *v.* to increase little by little; to expand

  It takes time to **develop** good ideas.

- **especially** *adv.* mainly; in particular

  The weather here is **especially** pleasant in summertime.

- **essential** *adj.* needed; necessary

  It is **essential** that everyone prepare for the exam.

- **globalized** *adj.* going across the entire world

  The world has become more **globalized** in recent years.

- **international** *adj.* involving two or more nations

  International trade in Europe is increasing a lot.

- **native language** *n.* the language a person learns from birth; a first language

His **native language** is Spanish, but he can speak three others.

- **require** *v.* to be in need of; to want

  I **require** quiet so that I can do the work well.

- **society** *n.* the system of community life

  Society has been changing for thousands of years.

- **subject** *n.* a course; an area of study

  The **subject** he enjoys learning the most is history.

- **successful** *adj.* wealthy; popular

  Ms. Jones is a **successful** woman who owns three businesses.

- **survey** *n.* a questioning of people to learn their opinions about a topic

  Please answer the questions on this short **survey**.

- **trouble** *n.* something that causes problems

  There is some **trouble** with the engine in the airplane.

- **value** *v.* to understand the importance of; to appreciate

  We **value** your contributions to the company.

- **widely** *adv.* across a large distance

  People **widely** agree that honesty is a very important characteristic.

Chapter 2

- **aware** *adj.* knowing about

  Are you **aware** of any problems with the report?

capture *v.* to catch

The hunters are trying to **capture** an alligator.

detect *v.* to see; to find, often after looking for something

I **detect** a slight increase in the amount of money we are making.

dive *v.* to go down deep in the water

Some animals can **dive** to the bottom of the ocean.

echolocation *n.* a system like sonar that animals use to detect and locate objects

Echolocation works like sonar for certain animals.

encounter *n.* a meeting

We do not want to have an **encounter** with a bear in the woods.

enormous *adj.* huge; very large

Skyscrapers are **enormous** buildings that rise high off the ground.

flee *v.* to run away; to try to escape from

The soldiers began to **flee** when the enemy forces appeared.

gather *v.* to collect

Solar panels **gather** light from the sun to make electricity.

hypothesize *v.* to believe; to come up with a theory

He will **hypothesize** on the matter after he looks at the data.

impressive *adj.* able to create a positive opinion

She had an **impressive** performance at the Olympics.

locate *v.* to find; to detect

We are trying to **locate** the key, but we cannot find it.

pitch black *adj.* very dark

It is impossible to drive when conditions are **pitch black**.

predator *n.* an animal that hunts other animals to kill and eat

Lions are some of the world's most dangerous **predators**.

prey *n.* an animal that is hunted by others for food

The hunters search for **prey** when they wake up.

range *n.* an extent

The weapon has a **range** of more than 500 meters.

rely *v.* to depend on

They **rely** on the bus to take them to school and home.

roughly *adv.* around; about

There are **roughly** 200 diamonds in the container.

survive *v.* to stay alive

It is impossible to **survive** in space without a spacesuit.

tentacle *n.* a long, slender appendage of an animal that is often used to taste or feel

The cook is preparing a meal with squid **tentacles**.

Chapter 3

debate *v.* to argue for or against something

They are **debating** which problem to solve next.

- **excellent** *adj.* very good of its kind; of the highest quality

  The chef at this restaurant makes **excellent** pasta dishes.

- **flaw** *n.* a mistake; an error

  Try to find the **flaw** in the solution you were given.

- **force** *n.* power; energy

  You must apply a lot of **force** to get the object to move.

- **fossil** *n.* the remains of a living thing from the distant past

  The paleontologists are digging up the dinosaur **fossil**.

- **gravity** *n.* the force that pulls objects toward a planet

  The **gravity** on Jupiter is stronger than it is on Earth.

- **hollow** *adj.* having empty space on the inside

  The wood rotted, so the tree trunk is **hollow** now.

- **hunter** *n.* an animal that chases other animals for food

  The **hunter** is setting traps for rabbits.

- **injure** *v.* to get hurt; to be harmed

  You will **injure** yourself if you are not careful.

- **mark** *n.* something that can be seen on an object

  There is a **mark** on the car where it was hit.

- **mass** *n.* the weight of an object

  The sun has the most **mass** of anything in the solar system.

- **perhaps** *adv.* maybe; possibly

  Perhaps we should see a movie this evening.

- **remain** *v.* to stay in the same condition

  He **remained** the same after ten years in another country.

- **risk** *n.* the possibility of suffering harm; danger

  There is always a **risk** of getting hurt when playing a game.

- **severe** *adj.* causing great damage; extreme

  Some of the side effects of the medicine can be **severe**.

Chapter 4

- **annually** *adv.* each year; once a year

  The city holds a spring festival **annually**.

- **crop** *n.* a plant that is grown to eat or use in other ways

  This year, the farmers are expecting a good corn **crop**.

- **damage** *v.* to harm

  You will **damage** the plate if you drop it.

- **decline** *v.* to go down; to become less in number or amount

  The price of gold has been **declining** recently.

- **excessive** *adj.* going beyond what is usual or necessary

  The fee for a late book at the library is **excessive**.

- **fallow** *adj.* not in use; plowed but unseeded, as in a field

  Animals are eating the grass in the **fallow** field.

- **fertile** *adj.* capable of being productive

  Plants can grow very well in **fertile** fields.

- **fertilizer** *n.* something added to make land more productive

  Some farmers prefer to add no **fertilizer** to their fields.

- **harvest** *v.* to gather ripe crops in a field

  They will **harvest** their crops in September and October.

- **infertile** *adj.* unable to produce anything

  This **infertile** land cannot grow anything on it.

- **multiple** *adj.* many

  Multiple people warned him to be careful.

- **nutrient** *n.* something that promotes growth and good health

  It is important to get enough **nutrients** on a daily basis.

- **propose** *v.* to suggest

  How do you **propose** that we solve this problem?

- **remove** *v.* to take out or away

  You need to **remove** the things from the room and clean it.

- **replace** *v.* to provide one thing as a substitute for another

  Let's **replace** the old batteries with some new ones.

- **rotate** *v.* to make something go through a cycle of changes

  It takes 24 hours for the Earth to **rotate** once.

- **soil** *n.* ground; dirt; earth

  The tractor is digging up the **soil** to get ready for planting.

- **starvation** *n.* the act of dying from a lack of food

  Starvation is still a big problem in many countries.

- **virtually** *adv.* nearly; almost

  There are **virtually** no people in the theater to watch the movie.

- **yield** *n.* the quantity or amount produced

  The **yield** on potatoes is much bigger than most other vegetables.

Chapter 5

- **carbon dating** *n.* a scientific process that measures how old an object is

  The scientists will use **carbon dating** to learn how old the artifact is.

- **century** *n.* a period of one hundred years

  There were many wars during the twentieth **century**.

- **ceremony** *n.* an act or set of acts done in a special way

  The school will hold its graduation **ceremony** next month.

- **common** *adj.* happening very often; usual

  The **common** cold can give people a sore throat.

- **construct** *v.* to create by putting together parts; to build

  It will take a couple of years to **construct** the new bridge.

- **countless** *adj.* too many to be counted; numerous

  Countless people were injured during the war.

- **descend** *v.* to be related to

  She claims that she is **descended** from a king of France.

- **document** *n.* a writing that provides information

  Please read the **document** completely before you sign it.

- **layout** *n.* the way something is organized; a design

  The **layout** of the house provides lots of room for everyone.

- **manmade** *adj.* made by human beings instead of nature; artificial

  Manmade dams can create big lakes behind them.

- **marsh** *n.* land that is wet and soft all the time

  All kinds of water birds lay their eggs in the **marsh**.

- **recently** *adv.* newly; lately

  Recently, the weather has been warmer than normal.

- **ritual** *n.* a set of acts done for religious reasons

  The **ritual** will be held in the temple this weekend.

- **seem** *v.* to appear to be true or likely

  It **seems** like Mr. Arnold is a generous man.

- **site** *n.* the place or setting of something

  This is the **site** of a building that was made in ancient times.

- **structure** *n.* something constructed, such as a building

  The **structure** has been designed to last for 100 years.

- **suggest** *v.* to offer up an idea or something to think about

  Please **suggest** something if you have any better ideas.

- **summer solstice** *n.* the time when the sun is farthest from the equator

  The **summer solstice** was important to people in many ancient cultures.

- **worship** *v.* to love or respect something deeply

  They go to church to **worship** every Sunday.

Chapter 6

- **average** *adj.* typical; common; usual

  The **average** person in that country lives until around eighty.

- **battery** *n.* a device that can store energy

  It is important to recharge the cellphone **battery** every day.

- **break down** *v.* to stop working; to fail

  The motor will **break down** if it is not taken care of.

- **efficient** *adj.* performing in the best way possible

  This is the most **efficient** way to repair the machine.

- **emission** *n.* something that is released into the air

  You cannot see some **emissions**, but they are still dangerous.

- **fee** *n.* a payment for a professional service

  The lawyer charges a high **fee** for his services.

- **inexpensive** *adj.* cheap; not costing a lot of money

  Many people prefer to purchase **inexpensive** clothes.

- **internal combustion engine** *n.* an engine that runs when fuel is burned

  This car has an **internal combustion engine** that runs on gas.

- **maintenance** *n.* the act of keeping something such as a machine in good condition

  By performing regular **maintenance**, the life of the engine can be extended.

- **mechanic** *n.* a person who fixes vehicles

  The **mechanic** is currently repairing a truck.

- **mining** *n.* the act of digging in the earth for rocks or minerals

  Gold **mining** can make people a lot of money in some countries.

- **poison** *v.* to kill or injure by using a harmful substance

  He was arrested for trying to **poison** another person.

- **pollutant** *n.* anything that makes the land, air, or water dirty

  There are many laws against releasing **pollutants** into the air.

- **power plant** *n.* a place that creates electricity

  The nuclear **power plant** produces cheap, clean energy,

- **recharge** *v.* to charge again with electricity

  It will take about thirty minutes to **recharge** the battery.

- **release** *v.* to let go; to send out

  They **released** the animals into the wild.

- **repair** *v.* to fix something that is broken

  Please try to **repair** the broken vase.

- **replacement** *n.* a substitute for a person or thing

  Mr. Simmons is the **replacement** for the sick teacher.

- **require** *v.* to need

  If you **require** assistance, please feel free to ask.

- **terrible** *adj.* very bad

  The weather has been **terrible** here lately.

- **address** *v.* to concentrate on; to focus on

  They will **address** the issues with the employees at the meeting.

- **advance** *v.* to move forward

  The general ordered the soldiers to **advance** on the city.

- **affect** *v.* to create a change in something

  The new rules **affect** everyone at the company.

- **astound** *v.* to impress strongly by something unexpected; to amaze

  She was **astounded** by his ability to work quickly.

- **bacteria** *n.* extremely small and simple animals

  Some **bacteria** can be very harmful to people.

- **bring about** *phr v.* to make something happen

  We hope to **bring about** changes sometime soon.

- **colonization** *n.* the act of making a home in a new place

  The **colonization** of North America began in the 1500s.

- **crowded** *adj.* filled as much as possible; cramped

  The subway can be very **crowded** during rush hour.

- **development** *n.* an improvement; a growth

  Her **development** as a student helped her grades improve.

- **donate** *v.* to give something as a gift

  He often **donates** money to help the homeless and the poor.

- **exist** *v.* to live; to be real

  Some people believe that ghosts and monsters **exist**.

- **exploration** *n.* the act of going to a place that one knows little about

  The **exploration** of the rainforest will take many years.

- **government** *n.* a system of ruling or controlling

  The **government** of that country does not listen to the people.

- **the human race** *n.* all human beings

  Many people hope that **the human race** will live on Mars one day.

- **key** *adj.* most important; significant

  Please find the **key** point in the passage.

- **modern** *adj.* of current times; present

  During **modern** times, there have been many technological advances.

- **poverty** *n.* the state of being poor; not having money

  Millions of people in that country live in **poverty**.

- **volcano** *n.* an opening in the earth where very hot rocks come out

  The **volcano** erupted and sent ash high into the sky.

Chapter 8

- **afford** *v.* to have enough money to pay for something

  I cannot **afford** to pay back the money that I owe him.

- **alternative energy source** *n.* energy that comes from the sun, wind, or water

  One popular **alternative energy source** is water.

- **constantly** *adv.* without stopping; continually

  The dog is **constantly** barking and will not be quiet.

- **drawback** *n.* a condition that makes something difficult; a disadvantage

  Name some of the **drawbacks** to the newest proposal.

- **forever** *adv.* for a limitless time; endlessly

  It is impossible for anyone to live **forever**.

- **gas** *n.* something not solid or liquid

  Water vapor is a very common greenhouse **gas**.

- **hidden cost** *n.* a disadvantage that is not known right away

  Always look for the **hidden costs** in the projects.

- **panel** *n.* a flat, rectangular piece of material

  You need to remove a **panel** to find the electric wires.

- **poison** *n.* something that causes illness or death

  Some animals can use **poison** as a defense.

- **pollution** *n.* something that harms living things and dirties the environment

  There is so much air **pollution** in many big cities.

- **sensitive** *adj.* easily hurt or damaged

  He has **sensitive** ears which can hurt when there are loud sounds.

- **solution** *n.* the answer to a problem

  Let's work together to find a **solution** to the problem.

- **supplement** *v.* to add to something to improve or complete it

  You can **supplement** your diet by taking various vitamins.

- **traditional energy source** *n.* coal, oil, or gas

  Most people around the world get heat from **traditional energy sources**.

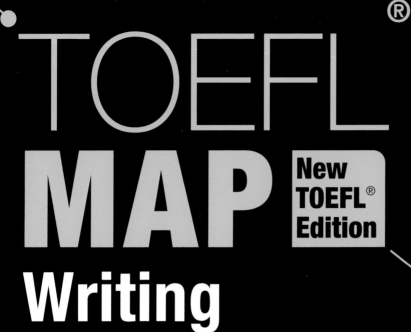

TOEFL MAP Writing

New TOEFL Edition

Basic

Scripts and Answer Key

TOEFL® MAP Writing

New TOEFL® Edition

Basic

Scripts and
Answer Key

 DARAKWON

Part A

 Introduction | **01** **Writing Section**

Information Organization Exercise
p.13

Answers may vary.

1
- **Thesis Statement** *My favorite season is summer.*
- **First Supporting Argument** *For one, summer has the best weather.*

   Detailed Supporting Example *I enjoy going to the beach with my family.*
- **Second Supporting Argument** *Moreover, I have less work to do during summer.*

   Detailed Supporting Example *I am on vacation during summer.*

2
- **Thesis Statement** *Children should not be allowed to play video games.*
- **First Supporting Argument** *The first reason is that playing games is not healthy.*

   Detailed Supporting Example *Children eat junk food and gain weight.*
- **Second Supporting Argument** *On top of this, games also do not allow children to develop social skills.*

   Detailed Supporting Example *Gamers spend less time talking with other people.*

 Introduction | **02** **Integrated Writing Section**

Summarizing and Paraphrasing
p.19

⊘ **Sample Summarizing and Paraphrasing Exercises**

Summarizing Exercise

Main Idea

The lecturer gives two reasons why animal testing *should be stopped*.

First Supporting Argument

For his first argument, the lecturer explains that animal testing is *not that helpful*. He says that animal testing usually does not produce *useful results*. The lecturer talks about one medicine that did not harm mice but made humans *very sick*.

Second Supporting Argument

The lecturer goes on to say that scientists have *alternative methods* to test products. One is using computer models for testing. Another is using *human cells*.

Paraphrasing Exercise   Answers may vary.

1 *The lecturer gives two reasons why animal testing must not continue.*

2 *The lecturer's first argument is that animal testing is not very useful.*

3 *He explains that animal testing often does not create valuable results.*

4 *The lecturer discusses one medicine that did not hurt mice but caused humans to become very ill.*

5 *The lecturer then explains that scientists have other ways to test products.*

Tandem Note-Taking
p.20

Answers may vary.

Reading	Listening
Main Idea	**Main Idea**
Animal testing is necessary for important advancements to occur.	*The professor argues that animal testing must not continue.*
First Supporting Argument	**First Supporting Argument**
Animal testing makes human lives better.	*Animal testing is not very useful.*
Supporting Detail	Supporting Detail
useful in making medicine	*medicine did not make mice sick but made humans sick*
Second Supporting Argument	**Second Supporting Argument**
Animal testing is an effective way to test products.	*Scientists have other ways to test products.*
Supporting Detail	Supporting Detail
some animals very similar to human beings	*using human cells; computer models*

Saample Response
p.22

[d] The reading passage argues that animal testing is necessary for important advancements to occur. [c] On the other hand, the professor feels that animal testing must not continue.

[b] The lecturer's first argument is that animal testing is not that useful. He claims that animal tests usually do not produce helpful results. [e] To explain this, the professor talks about one medicine tested on mice. The medicine did not make the mice sick. However, it made people very sick. [a] This contrasts the idea given in the reading passage. It argues that animal testing makes human lives better. It states that it is useful in making medicine.

[b] For his second argument, the speaker states that

scientists have other ways to test products. [e] One of these ways is using human cells. This is beneficial because it does not hurt living creatures. It is also more accurate than testing animals. Another method is using computer modeling. [a] The passage makes a different argument. It states that animal testing is the best way to test products. The reason is that some animals are very similar to human beings.

 Introduction | 03 Independent Writing Section

Understanding the Background
p.26

⊘ **Sample Understanding the Background Exercise**
Answers may vary.

1   People your age might be experiencing the *same problems* as you.

2   Older people better understand the *effects* of a decision.

3   People who are older may have faced *similar problems* when they were younger.

4   Getting *dating advice* from an older person might be awkward.

5   Someone who is older has *more knowledge* than a younger person.

6   Older people are more likely to understand how a bad decision can affect your life *later on*.

7   Your peers are more likely to *understand your situation* better.

8   Asking younger people is usually better for *social matters*.

Selecting and Generating Ideas
p.27

⊘ **Sample Selecting Ideas Exercise**
Answers may vary.

Agree:

- It is often better to get advice from older people. *(Topic Sentence)*

- Older people generally have more life experience.

- People who are older can better understand the long-term effects of a decision.

Disagree:

- There are some situations when it is better to ask your peers for advice. *(Topic Sentence)*

- People your age will probably understand your

situation better.

- Asking peers for social advice is usually more comfortable.

⊘ **Sample Generating Ideas Exercise**
Answers may vary.

Agree:

1   Getting advice from older people is *often better*.

2   People who are older have more *life experience* than younger people.

3   Older people can understand how a decision can affect your life in the *long term*.

Disagree:

1   In some situations, getting advice *from your peers* is more valuable.

2   Your peers are more likely to understand *your situation*.

3   Asking people your age for advice can be *more comfortable*.

Outlining Exercise
p.28

Planning
Answers may vary.

Agree	Disagree
Thesis Statement	**Thesis Statement**
I strongly believe that getting advice from older people is better.	*To me, it seems that getting advice from my peers is more valuable.*
First Supporting Idea	**First Supporting Idea**
People who are older have more life experience.	*Your peers are more likely to understand your situation.*
Supporting Example	Supporting Example
experienced similar things when younger	*recently had similar experience; got driver's license*
Second Supporting Idea	**Second Supporting Idea**
Older people can understand how a decision can affect your life long term.	*Asking people your age for social advice can be more comfortable.*
Supporting Example	Supporting Example
going to college; quitting school	*getting dating advice*
Conclusion	**Conclusion**
In conclusion, it is better to get advice from people who are older.	*I believe getting advice from my peers is a better idea in most situations.*

Sample Response

p.30

[b] When faced with a difficult situation, it is important to get advice from other people. Some people may feel that getting advice from someone older is best. [d] As for me, I think getting advice from people the same age is more valuable.

[f] To begin with, your peers are more likely to understand your problem. [c] They might have recently experienced a similar situation. This means that they can give you more appropriate advice. [e] This is what happened when I tried to get my driver's license. I wanted to know what the driving test was like. So I asked my friends about it. Many of them had recently gotten their driver's licenses. They were therefore able to give me advice about the same situation.

[f] Furthermore, getting advice from people your own age can be more comfortable. [c] It is easier to talk about some things with your peers than with people who are older. [e] In my case, I chose to ask my friends for advice on dating. I asked them what I should do on a date and what I should avoid doing. Of course, older people have gone on dates before. But talking about dating with a teacher or a parent is awkward. For sensitive topics, I feel that getting advice from my peers is better.

[a] Getting advice is the best way to make intelligent decisions. There may be certain times when getting advice from an older person is better. [g] However, for the reasons given, I believe getting advice from peers is a better idea in most situations.

Part B

● Chapter | 01 Integrated Writing

Linguistics: Learning a Foreign Language

Vocabulary
p.34

1 widely
2 especially
3 Society
4 Successful
5 globalized
6 communicate
7 essential
8 conduct
9 value
10 international

▮ Reading
p.35

Summarizing

Main Idea

The author of the reading passage believes that students should study *foreign languages*. The reason is that being able to communicate with people from *around the world* is very important in business.

First Supporting Argument

The first argument the author gives is that companies need employees who can speak a *second language*. The reason is that these companies do *international business*.

Second Supporting Argument

The author's next reason is that learning a foreign language helps students get *good jobs*. Employers understand that foreign languages are *essential for business*.

Vocabulary
p.36

1 native language
2 concentrate
3 bank teller
4 subject
5 requires

6 surveys
7 develop
8 trouble

Listening
p.37

Script
02-01

M: Now listen to part of a lecture on the topic you just read about.

Professor: Let's take a quick survey. How many of you are studying a foreign language? Just raise your hands . . . All right. Nearly all of you. I do believe that learning is a good thing. But I also feel that other subjects are more important than foreign languages. Allow me to explain.

To begin with, many students have trouble reading and writing in their own language. They can't read passages well or express themselves clearly. So these students should concentrate on developing their native language skills first. They need to be able to use their native language well. Otherwise, they will not be able to go to university. And this is the most important factor for getting a good job and for being successful in life.

What's more, many jobs do not require foreign language skills anyway. For instance, people looking for jobs as bank tellers do not need to speak another language. The reason is that all their customers will speak the same language. Since this is true with most jobs, it is extremely important for students to develop other more useful skills. These include math, science, and computer skills.

Summarizing

Main Idea

The professor explains that students should study *other subjects* rather than study a foreign language.

First Supporting Argument

First, she argues that most children cannot read or write their *native language* very well. Therefore, they need to *concentrate on developing* these skills first.

Second Supporting Argument

The professor also believes that knowing a foreign language is *not needed* for most jobs. She gives the example of a(n) *bank teller*. Overall, the professor *is against* the idea of learning a foreign language.

Paraphrasing Exercise
p.38

Reading
Answers may vary.

1 *The writer of the reading passage thinks that students should study foreign languages.*

2 *The author's first supporting argument is that companies need workers who know a foreign language.*

3 *The reason is that these companies do business in foreign countries.*

4 *Next, the author argues that studying a second language helps students find good jobs.*

5 *Employers realize that foreign languages are necessary for business.*

Listening
Answers may vary.

1 *The instructor argues that students should learn about other subjects rather than study a second language.*

2 *Her first argument is that most students cannot use their native language very well.*

3 *For this reason, students need to focus on developing their native language abilities first.*

4 *Next, the professor states that speaking a foreign language is not needed for most jobs.*

5 *On the whole, the professor does not support the idea of studying a second language.*

Tandem Note-Taking
p.39
Answers may vary.

Reading	Listening
Main Idea	**Main Idea**
Students need to learn a foreign language to be successful in today's world.	*Students should focus on other subjects rather than learn a second language.*
First Supporting Argument	**First Supporting Argument**
Businesses need employees who can speak a foreign language.	*Most students are not able to use their first language very well.*
Supporting Detail	Supporting Detail
especially true when a country's language is not widely spoken	*cannot get a good job or go to college*

Second Supporting Argument	Second Supporting Argument
Knowing a foreign language helps students get good jobs.	*Most jobs do not require foreign language skills.*
Supporting Detail	Supporting Detail
can get good jobs more easily; can also earn more money	*bank tellers do not need a foreign language; customers speak the same language*

▇ Sample Response

Critical Analysis

1 Ⓑ

2 Ⓒ

3 develop

4 on the other hand

● Chapter | **01** Independent Writing

Teaching Responsibility with Pets

▇ Background & Brainstorming

p.42

Understanding the Background
Answers may vary.

1 Children can learn about responsibility by *caring* for a pet.

2 Sometimes young children may not understand how to *treat* their pets properly.

3 Children learn that animals have *feelings* from their pets.

4 Pets can *get hurt* and need to go the hospital just like people do.

5 Many children do not have a lot of *patience*, so they do not care for their pets.

6 Caring for a pet can teach children how to be *responsible adults* and good parents.

7 *Parents* may have to care for the pets instead of their children.

8 Children learn that animals need *food and water* regularly.

Selecting Ideas

Agree

• Caring for a pet is a great way to teach children about responsibility. *(Topic Sentence)*

• Pets will not survive without receiving food and water from their owners.

• Children learn about taking care of another living creature.

Disagree

• Children should learn about responsibility in other ways. *(Topic Sentence)*

• Many children are too young to handle pets properly.

• Many parents of young children usually end up caring for the pet.

Generating Ideas
Answers may vary.

Agree

1 Children must give their pets *food and water* regularly in order for them to survive.

2 Pets teach children how to care for another *living creature*.

3 Caring for a pet is an excellent way to teach children about *responsibility*.

Disagree

1 There are *other ways* to teach children about responsibility.

2 Children that are too young cannot *handle* pets properly.

3 Parents with young children usually end up *caring* for the pet instead.

▇ Planning

p.44

Answers may vary.

Agree	Disagree
Thesis Statement	**Thesis Statement**
I feel that the best way to teach children about responsibility is by caring for an animal.	*I believe there are better ways to teach responsibility than caring for an animal.*
First Supporting Idea	**First Supporting Idea**
Pets teach children how to care for a living creature.	*Young children are not able to handle pets properly.*

give food and water each day

Second Supporting Idea

Children learn that animals have feelings.

Supporting Example

must keep pet happy

Conclusion

Having a pet is a great way for children to learn about responsibility.

Supporting Example

can hurt the pet

Second Supporting Idea

Parents usually take care of the pet for their children.

Supporting Example

parents feed pet; walk it

Conclusion

Children should learn about responsibility in other ways.

First Supporting Argument

First, the passage claims that the squids' eyes are useful when they hunt. The giant squid can *dive deep* beneath the surface, where it is very dark. The eyes *gather light* and let the squid see so that they can hunt.

Second Supporting Argument

The passage goes on to mention that *sperm whales* hunt giant squid. So squid need *strong eyesight* to help them detect sperm whales. It states that squid can *flee or fight* whenever they see a sperm whale.

Sample Response   p.46

Critical Analysis

1 Ⓑ

2 Ⓒ

3 but

● Chapter | 02 Integrated Writing

Zoology: The Eyes of the Giant Squid

Vocabulary   p.48

1 flee
2 hypothesize
3 gathers
4 detect
5 impressive
6 encounter
7 dive
8 survive
9 roughly
10 predators

Reading   p.49

Summarizing

Main Idea

The reading passage states that giant squid have *a huge eye* on each side of their head.

Vocabulary   p.50

1 locate
2 tentacles
3 pitch black
4 Echolocation
5 capture
6 enormous
7 range
8 aware
9 Prey
10 rely on

Listening   p.51

Script   02-02

M: Now listen to part of a lecture on the topic you just read about.

Professor: This is a picture of a giant squid. As you can see, it has two enormous eyes. Why are its eyes so big? That's something we don't know the answer to.

Some scientists have theories, but each has some problems. For instance, a few scientists claim the eyes are necessary for the giant squid to hunt. Unfortunately, I don't believe that's correct. You see, giant squid do most of their hunting hundreds or even thousands of meters beneath the surface. That deep, there's no sunlight, so it's pitch black. The squid doesn't rely on its eyes to hunt when it's down so deep. Instead, it utilizes its tentacles to feel. When the squid touches prey, it grabs the animal with its tentacles to capture it.

There are also theories that the eyes are necessary to locate sperm whales, yet I don't consider that true. Yes, the squid can see things more than 100 meters away. However, sperm whales use echolocation to hunt. So they can detect prey, including giant squid, from a much greater distance. It's believed that their echolocation has a range of around 300 meters. So sperm whales are aware of giant squid long before the squid know the whales are around.

Summarizing

Main Idea

In the lecture, the instructor believes that the theories on *the purposes* of the eyes of giant squid have problems. He gives two reasons to support his argument.

First Supporting Argument

The instructor's first argument is that giant squid hunt in places *with no light*. Therefore, their eyes cannot help them see well enough to hunt. Instead, the instructor remarks that squid use *their tentacles* when they hunt.

Second Supporting Argument

Next, the instructor states that sperm whales *use echolocation*. As a result, they can detect giant squid *from far away*. This means that they *are aware of* giant squid long before the squid know the whales are around.

▪ Paraphrasing Exercise   p.52

Reading
Answers may vary.

1 The reading passage states that giant squid have a huge eye on <u>both</u> sides of their head.

2 First, the passage mentions that the squids' eyes are useful when it is searching for <u>prey</u>.

3 The eyes <u>collect</u> light, so the squid can see well enough to hunt.

4 The passage next mentions that sperm whales try to <u>kill</u> and eat giant squid.

5 It states that squid can <u>escape</u> or fight if they encounter a sperm whale.

Listening
Answers may vary.

1 In the lecture, the instructor comments that each theory on the purpose of giant squid eyes is <u>wrong</u>.

2 The instructor's first argument is that giant squid hunt in <u>dark</u> places.

3 Rather, the instructor remarks that squid use their tentacles when searching for <u>prey</u>.

4 Next, the instructor <u>remarks</u> that sperm whales use echolocation.

5 As a result, they can find giant squid from great <u>distances</u>.

▪ Tandem Note-Taking   p.53

Answers may vary.

Reading	Listening
Main Idea	**Main Idea**
The huge eyes of the giant squid have a couple of purposes.	*The theories on the purposes of the eyes of giant squid have problems.*
First Supporting Argument	**First Supporting Argument**
The eyes help squid see well enough to hunt in dark water.	*Giant squid hunt in dark places.*
Supporting Detail	Supporting Detail
dive deep; very dark; eyes gather light; can see better	*eyes cannot help them see; use tentacles for hunting*
Second Supporting Argument	**Second Supporting Argument**
The eyes let squid detect sperm whales that are hunting them.	*Sperm whales can detect giant squid by using echolocation.*
Supporting Detail	Supporting Detail
strong eyesight helps them find sperm whales; can flee or fight	*can find squid from far away; know about squid before squid know the whales are there*

▪ Sample Response   p.55

Critical Analysis

1 (B)

2 (A)

3 disregards

4 so, instead

● Chapter | 02 Independent Writing

Young People Need More Exercise

■ Background & Brainstorming   p.56

Understanding the Background
Answers may vary.

1   In past years, children *used to walk* to school and played outside.

2   Doctors worry that children do not know the *value* of staying healthy.

3   Schools have *physical education* classes to make sure that children get exercise.

4   Not everyone believes that children need to worry about *losing weight*.

5   Many foods young people eat today are high in *fat and calories*.

6   Today's young people do not get enough *exercise*.

7   Many children are *active and healthy* while only a few are overweight.

8   Some believe that *exercise programs* are too difficult for children to do by themselves.

Selecting Ideas

Agree

•   Young people today need to get more exercise. *(Topic Sentence)*

•   Today's young people have unhealthy lifestyles.

•   Children eat foods that are not good for them.

Disagree

•   Children are too young to worry about losing weight. *(Topic Sentence)*

•   Most children stay busy and are in good health.

•   Exercise programs can be dangerous for children.

Generating Ideas
Answers may vary.

Agree

1   Today's young people do not *exercise* often enough.

2   Young people eat foods that are *unhealthy*.

3   Children these days do not live *healthy lives*.

Disagree

1   Young people are not *old enough* to think about weight loss.

2   Children can *harm* themselves if they exercise.

3   Young people are usually *busy* and already healthy.

■ Planning   p.58
Answers may vary.

Agree	Disagree
Thesis Statement	**Thesis Statement**
It is my opinion that young children do not get enough exercise these days.	*I contend that children are not old enough to worry about losing weight.*
First Supporting Idea	**First Supporting Idea**
Young people do not live healthy lives.	*Most children stay busy and are in good health.*
Supporting Example	Supporting Example
do not walk to school; play computer games	*physical education classes; physical activities*
Second Supporting Idea	**Second Supporting Idea**
Young people eat unhealthy foods.	*Exercising can be dangerous.*
Supporting Example	Supporting Example
snacks, fast food, and other high-calorie foods	*too young to exercise properly*
Conclusion	**Conclusion**
Today's young people need to get more exercise.	*I believe that children are too young worry about weight loss.*

■ Sample Response   p.60

Critical Analysis

1   Ⓑ

2   Ⓐ

3   first of all, furthermore, in actuality

● Chapter | 03 Integrated Writing

Biology: Could Tyrannosaurus Rex Run?

Vocabulary   p.62

1   hunters

2   force

3 mass

4 remain

5 severe

6 Perhaps

7 gravity

8 injure

Reading

p.63

Summarizing

Main Idea

The reading passage argues that Tyrannosaurus rex *could not run*.

First Supporting Argument

One supporting idea given is that Tyrannosaurus rex was *too heavy* to run. Its *bones* were not strong enough to allow it run. If a Tyrannosaurus rex fell while running, it would have suffered a *severe injury*.

Second Supporting Argument

The second supporting idea is that Tyrannosaurus rex did not have large enough *leg muscles* to run. Its leg muscles were *twenty-five percent* of its mass. But it would have needed muscles larger than *fifty percent* of its mass to run.

Vocabulary

p.64

1 risks

2 mark

3 flaw

4 debated

5 excellent

6 hollow

7 fossils

Listening

p.65

Script

02-03

M: Now listen to part of a lecture on the topic you just read about.

Professor: There is no doubt that Tyrannosaurus rex was an excellent hunter. What is less certain is whether or not a T. rex could run. Personally, I believe that Tyrannosaurus rex was able to run.

Some people argue that T. rex could not run because it was so heavy. Yes, T. rex was a heavy animal. However, scientists now believe that it had hollow bones just like birds do. If this is true, then the animal would have been much lighter. It probably would have weighed fewer than five tons. This means that a Tyrannosaurus would have been able to run without the risk of injury.

Another popular argument is that T. rex did not have large enough leg muscles for running. There is one flaw with this argument: Nobody knows how large a T. rex's leg muscles really were. Thus, it is possible that T. rex was capable of running. What's more is that scientists have found fossils from other dinosaurs that have bite marks from Tyrannosauruses. Some of these dinosaurs were very fast. Therefore, to catch these animals, T. rex also must have been fast.

Summarizing

Main Idea

In the lecture, the speaker gives reasons why she thinks Tyrannosaurus rex *could run*.

First Supporting Argument

Her first argument deals with the dinosaur's weight. She says that a Tyrannosaurus had *hollow bones*. Therefore, it was *light enough* to run without the risk of injury.

Second Supporting Argument

For her second argument, the speaker claims that *nobody knows* how large the leg muscles of a Tyrannosaurus rex were. Moreover, she says that fossils from a fast animal had *bite marks* from a Tyrannosaurus. Due to this, the dinosaur was probably *able to run*.

Paraphrasing Exercise

p.66

Reading

Answers may vary.

1 *The author of the reading passage believes that Tyrannosaurus rex was not able to run.*

2 *The first supporting argument is that a Tyrannosaurus rex had too much mass to run.*

3   A Tyrannosaurus rex would have suffered *great harm* if it fell while running.

4   The next argument states that the leg muscles of a Tyrannosaurus rex were *too small* for it to run.

5   However, its muscles would have needed to be greater than *half of its total* weight.

Listening

Answers may vary.

1   The speaker presents arguments *supporting the idea* that Tyrannosaurus rex was able to run.

2   The speaker claims that the bones had *empty spaces* on their insides.

3   As a result, it was light enough to run without the possibility of *getting hurt*.

4   The speaker's second supporting idea is that *no one is sure* about the size of a Tyrannosaurus rex's leg muscles.

5   This suggests that the dinosaur was *capable* of running.

Tandem Note-Taking   p.67

Answers may vary.

Reading	Listening
Main Idea	**Main Idea**
Tyrannosaurus rex was not able to run.	Tyrannosaurus rex was able to run.
First Supporting Argument	**First Supporting Argument**
Tyrannosaurus rex could not run because it had too much mass.	The bones of a Tyrannosaurus rex were actually empty on the inside.
Supporting Detail	Supporting Detail
bones were not strong enough; would have been severely injured	weighed fewer than five tons; could run without the possibility of getting hurt
Second Supporting Argument	**Second Supporting Argument**
Tyrannosaurus rex was not able to run because its leg muscles were not strong enough.	Nobody knows the size of a Tyrannosaurus rex's leg muscles.
Supporting Detail	Supporting Detail
leg muscles not greater than half its body mass	bite marks on the fossils of fast animals

Sample Response   p.69

Critical Analysis

1   Ⓒ

2   Ⓐ

3   flawed

4   in contrast, additionally

● Chapter | 03 **Independent Writing**

Visiting Historical Sites or Restaurants and Cafés

Background & Brainstorming   p.70

Understanding the Background

Answers may vary.

1   The archaeologists found some *artifacts* at the dig site.

2   The Renaissance was a great *time period* in Europe.

3   Many eating *establishments* in the city serve seafood.

4   The tourist plan to *explore* the museum later in the day.

5   Some of the *artwork* made by the painters is impressive.

6   Let's have a *meal* that includes some traditional Spanish food.

7   There are plenty of *historical sites* to see in France.

8   They saw paintings and sculptures at those *art galleries* last week.

Selecting Ideas

Visiting Historical Sites

•   Some people like learning about the past by going to various places in cities. *(Topic Sentence)*

•   It can be educational to see artifacts from a city's past.

•   A lot about a culture can be learned by studying its history.

Spending Time at Restaurants and Cafés

•   Some people prefer to relax and enjoy a meal when

they go somewhere new. *(Topic Sentence)*

- It is fun to sample new foods and to see how people in other places eat.
- Not everyone likes to spend all of their time on their feet.

Generating Ideas

Answers may vary.

Visiting Historical Sites

1 There are *various places* in cities that people can see to learn about the past.

2 A person can learn about a country's *culture* by studying its past.

3 Examining *artifacts* from a city's past is educational.

Spending Time at Restaurants and Cafés

1 Spending time on *their feet* is not fun for everyone.

2 Some people prefer to *enjoy meals* when they visit new cities.

3 *Sampling new foods* is one way to learn about a new city.

■ Planning   p.72

Answers may vary.

Visiting Historical Sites	Spending Time at Restaurants and Cafés
Thesis Statement *A lot of people like to learn about the past by going to historical sites in cities.*	**Thesis Statement** *Many people enjoy spending time at restaurants and cafés when they visit foreign cities.*
First Supporting Idea *It can be an educational experience to see artifacts from a city's past.*	**First Supporting Idea** *I love to sample new foods from foreign places to see how people eat.*
Supporting Example *look at artifacts; see how people once lived*	Supporting Example *try new foods; try to eat foods that the natives of the country eat*
Second Supporting Idea *People can also learn about another culture by studying the history of a place.*	**Second Supporting Idea** *Many people prefer to stay off their feet in foreign cities and have more relaxed trips.*
Supporting Example *history tells how people developed; can understand how culture developed over time*	Supporting Example *don't have to be on feet all day; can meet natives more easily*

Conclusion	Conclusion
I prefer to visit historical sites when I visit a foreign city than to spend time at restaurants and cafés.	*I prefer to spend time at restaurants and cafés when I visit a foreign city than to visit historical sites.*

■ Sample Response   p.74

Critical Analysis

1 Ⓐ

2 Ⓑ

3 but, in addition

● Chapter | 04 Integrated Writing

Agriculture: The Pros and Cons of Using Fertilizer

Vocabulary   p.76

1 fertile

2 Starvation

3 multiple

4 soil

5 crops

6 Nutrients

7 harvest

8 fertilizer

9 yield

10 annually

■ Reading   p.77

Summarizing

Main Idea

The reading passage deals with the issue of *using fertilizer*. The reading passage states that it provides *many benefits*.

First Supporting Argument

The passage first argues that fertilizer can increase *the crop yield* for farmers. It adds nutrients such as nitrogen, potassium, and phosphorous to the soil. As a result, the yields of crops like *corn and wheat* increase.

Second Supporting Argument

Next, the passage explains that fertilizer lets farmers get multiple crop yields every year. Because there are _enough nutrients_ in the soil, farmers can get two crops of the same or different plants. This helps reduce the _threat of starvation_.

Vocabulary p.78

1   declines
2   rotates
3   damaged
4   fallow
5   virtually
6   propose
7   remove
8   Infertile
9   Replace
10 excessive

▌ Listening p.79

Script   02-04

M: Now listen to part of a lecture on the topic you just read about.

Professor: We all know about the benefits of fertilizer. But some people oppose using it. They propose different ways of taking care of the soil. I see their point regarding some of their arguments.

Too much fertilizer can be a bad thing. Every year, some farmers put enormous amounts of fertilizer on their fields. This adds much-needed nutrients. Yet it can damage the soil. Studies show that excessive use of fertilizer can harm the land. This doesn't happen in the short term though. It happens over a period of thirty or so years. Once the land is damaged, the number of crops that can grow on it declines. Over time, the land can become infertile, so virtually nothing grows on it.

Instead of adding fertilizer, some people propose using crop rotation. Basically, each year, farmers change the crops they grow in their fields. For instance, some farmers use the three-field system. Let's say they have three fields. In one field, they grow wheat. In another, they grow peas. In another, they grow nothing. Each year, they rotate fields.

You see, wheat removes nutrients from the ground while peas replace them. And leaving fields fallow helps the soil become healthier. That's much better than growing multiple crops in the same field every year.

Summarizing

Main Idea

The lecturer explains that fertilizer can be _harmful to soil_. He adds that there are other ways to _take care of it_.

First Supporting Argument

The lecturer first argues that too much fertilizer can _damage the soil_. This takes place after around thirty years. When the soil is damaged, the land can _become infertile_.

Second Supporting Argument

The lecturer next mentions that crop rotation can help the soil instead of adding fertilizer. Farmers _rotate the crops_ they grow in their fields by using the _three-field system_. Then, the soil can become healthier.

▌ Paraphrasing Exercise p.80

Reading
Answers may vary.

1   _The reading passage deals with the_ topic _of using fertilizer._

2   _The passage first argues that fertilizer can_ improve _the crop yield for farmers._

3   _It adds nutrients such as nitrogen, potassium, and phosphorous to the_ earth.

4   _Next, the passage explains that fertilizer allows farmers to_ grow _more than one crop every year._

5   _This helps_ decrease _the threat of starvation._

Listening
Answers may vary.

1   _The lecturer states that fertilizer can be_ bad _for soil._

2   _His first argument is that using too much fertilizer can_ cause _problems for the soil._

3 *When the soil is harmed, the land can become <u>unproductive</u>.*

4 *The lecturer next mentions that crop rotation can help the soil <u>rather than</u> adding fertilizer.*

5 *Farmers <u>change</u> the crops they grow in their fields by using the three-field system.*

▓ Tandem Note-Taking p.81

Answers may vary.

Reading	Listening
Main Idea	**Main Idea**
Fertilizer provides many benefits to fields.	*Fertilizer can be harmful to the soil.*
First Supporting Argument	**First Supporting Argument**
Fertilizer can improve the crop yield of fields.	*Too much fertilizer can cause damage to the soil.*
Supporting Detail	Supporting Detail
adds nutrients such as nitrogen, potassium, and phosphorous; corn and wheat yields increase	*damage takes place over thirty years; land becomes infertile*
Second Supporting Argument	**Second Supporting Argument**
Farmers can get multiple crop yields each year by using fertilizer.	*Crop rotation is a better way to help the soil.*
Supporting Detail	Supporting Detail
soil has enough nutrients; can get two crops; reduces the threat of starvation	*rotate crops grown in fields; use three-field system; soil becomes healthier*

▓ Sample Response p.83

Critical Analysis

1 ⓒ

2 Ⓑ

3 tremendous

4 then

Students Should Not Have Part-Time Jobs

▓ Background & Brainstorming p.84

Understanding the Background

Answers may vary.

1 A lot of college students want to *earn money* and live independently.

2 Students can get unnecessary *stress* from part-time jobs.

3 With jobs, students do not need to *rely on* their parents for money.

4 Part-time jobs teach students how to *balance* work time with study time.

5 Students who work often have *lower grades* than students who do not work.

6 Part-time jobs usually do not pay *much money*.

7 Most college students have too much *schoolwork* to work at any part-time jobs.

8 Part-time jobs can give students *practical* job skills.

Selecting Ideas

Agree

- Having a part-time job can cause college students a lot of problems. *(Topic Sentence)*
- Most part-time jobs do not pay very high salaries.
- Students with jobs often have worse grades than students who do not.

Disagree

- Having a part-time job is a great way for students to solve their money problems. *(Topic Sentence)*
- Students with jobs learn how to make good use of their time.
- Part-time jobs also give students practical job skills.

Generating Ideas

Answers may vary.

Agree

1 Part-time jobs sometimes create *problems* for college students.

2 Students who work cannot focus on their *schoolwork* and often get worse grades.

3 Salaries at part-time jobs are usually not *very high*.

Disagree

1 Students can fix their *money problems* by having a part-time job.

2 Students learn how to make *good use* of their time by having a part-time job.

3 Doing a part-time job can teach students practical *job skills*.

Planning
p.86

Answers may vary.

Agree	Disagree
Thesis Statement	**Thesis Statement**
Having a part-time job sometimes creates problems for college students.	*Part-time jobs allow students to fix their money problems.*
First Supporting Idea	**First Supporting Idea**
Students who work cannot focus on their classwork.	*Students learn about life outside of education.*
Supporting Example	Supporting Example
lower grades; may not graduate on time or at all	*deal with managers; learn how to earn money*
Second Supporting Idea	**Second Supporting Idea**
Most part-time jobs do not have very high salaries.	*Students learn how to manage their time well.*
Supporting Example	Supporting Example
still need to borrow money from parents; not worth the risk of lower grades	*have to manage work and class schedules*
Conclusion	**Conclusion**
I believe that students should focus on their studies instead of doing part-time jobs.	*I feel that college students greatly benefit from having part-time jobs.*

Sample Response
p.88

Critical Analysis

1 Ⓒ

2 Ⓑ

3 however

Archaeology: The Builders of Stonehenge

Vocabulary
p.90

1 ritual

2 suggest

3 constructing

4 summer solstice

5 descended

6 layout

7 century

8 document

9 site

10 countless

Reading
p.91

Summarizing

Main Idea

In the reading passage, the author gives two arguments to explain that the *Druids constructed* Stonehenge.

First Supporting Argument

For the opening argument, the author states that the Druids were probably the *first people* to live around Stonehenge. The writer supports this by explaining that Stonehenge was constructed to pay respect to the *Celtic queen Boudicca*.

Second Supporting Argument

The next argument is that Stonehenge's layout *perfectly fits* with Druid rituals. Stonehenge tracks the points where the sun and the moon *rise and set*. It is therefore likely that the Druids used the site to *follow events* occurring in the sky.

Vocabulary
p.92

1 seems

2 manmade

3 ceremony

4 structure

5 recently

6 carbon dating

7 common

8 marshes

9 worship

Listening   p.93

Script   02-05

M: Now listen to part of a lecture on the topic you just read about.

Professor: Now, I'd like to tell you more about the construction of Stonehenge.

We all know that Stonehenge is a very old structure. But for years, no one knew exactly how old it was. That has changed. A group of scientists recently used carbon dating to figure out how old Stonehenge is. They found that the first Stonehenge structures were built around the year 3,000 B.C. This is more than 2,000 years before the Celts first went to England. For this reason, it seems clear to me that the Druids could not have built Stonehenge. It must have been built by an earlier people.

Oh, and there's also a debate about who used the site for rituals. Some people believe that the Druids used Stonehenge to hold most of their ceremonies. But if you examine the situation more closely, you'll find that this is not the case. You see, the Druids worshiped nature. They usually worshiped in natural places, such as forests and marshes. They would not have used manmade places for worship. This means that the Druids probably did not have a long connection with Stonehenge.

Summarizing

Main Idea

The professor gives reasons to explain why the Druids *did not build* Stonehenge.

First Supporting Argument

To start off, the professor explains that scientists used *carbon dating* to figure out how old Stonehenge is. They found that its structures were built more than *2,000 years* before the Celts went to England.

Second Supporting Argument

The professor then goes over the debate about the use of the site *for rituals*. She believes that the Druids did not worship in *manmade places*. This means that the Druids did not have a *long connection* with Stonehenge.

Paraphrasing Exercise   p.94

Reading
Answers may vary.

1 *The reading passage presents two reasons explaining that the Druids built Stonehenge.*

2 *The first supporting idea is that the Druids were probably the first people to stay around Stonehenge.*

3 *To strengthen this idea, the author states that Stonehenge was built to honor the Celtic queen Boudicca.*

4 *The second argument is that the design of Stonehenge matches Druid religious acts.*

5 *Therefore, the Druids probably used the location to track events happening in the sky.*

Listening
Answers may vary.

1 *The professor presents arguments to explain that the Druids did not construct Stonehenge.*

2 *To begin with, the professor says that researchers used carbon dating to determine the actual age of Stonehenge.*

3 *They discovered that the site was completed more than 2,000 years before the Celts arrived in England.*

4 *She feels that the Druids would not have worshiped in artificial places.*

5 *Therefore, it is unlikely that the Druids had a long connection with Stonehenge.*

Tandem Note-Taking   p.95
Answers may vary.

Reading	Listening
Main Idea	**Main Idea**
The Druids constructed Stonehenge.	*Stonehenge was not built by the Druids.*
First Supporting Argument	**First Supporting Argument**
The Druids were among the first people to stay around Stonehenge.	*Scientists used carbon dating to determine the actual age of Stonehenge.*
Supporting Detail	Supporting Detail
was built to honor a Celtic queen	*completed nearly 2,000 years before the Celts moved to England*

Second Supporting Argument	Second Supporting Argument
The design of Stonehenge matches Druid religious acts.	*The Druids would not have worshiped in places such as Stonehenge.*
Supporting Detail	Supporting Detail
tracks events happening in the sky	*actually worshiped in natural places*

■ Sample Response   p.97

Critical Analysis

1 Ⓒ

2 Ⓑ

3 artificial

4 on the other hand

● Chapter │ 05 Independent Writing

Parents Should Make Decisions for Their Children

■ Background & Brainstorming   p.98

Understanding the Background

Answers may vary.

1 Children do not have enough *knowledge and experience* to make the best decisions.

2 Having children make *important decisions* also has its drawbacks.

3 Making important decisions allows children to *mature* more quickly.

4 Most children do not think of the *long-term effects* of their decisions.

5 Making decisions teaches children how the choices they make *affect their lives*.

6 Parents almost always attempt to do *what is best* for their children.

7 Children cannot make good decisions because they are *too young*.

8 Important decisions can *change the lives* of children.

Selecting Ideas

Agree

- Allowing children to make important decisions has serious drawbacks. *(Topic Sentence)*
- Children often do not think about the long-term effects of their choices.
- Children do not possess enough experience and knowledge to make proper decisions.

Disagree

- Children can benefit from making important decisions on their own. *(Topic Sentence)*
- Children gain experience making decisions at a young age.
- The lives of children can greatly change because of important decisions.

Generating Ideas

Answers may vary.

Agree

1 There are *serious drawbacks* to allowing children to make important decisions.

2 Making important decisions requires *experience and knowledge* that children lack.

3 Children usually fail to think about the *long-term effects* of their decisions.

Disagree

1 Allowing children to make important decisions *benefits* them.

2 Important decisions can *greatly change* the lives of children.

3 Children can *gain experience* by making decisions when they are young.

■ Planning   p.100

Answers may vary.

Agree	Disagree
Thesis Statement	**Thesis Statement**
Allowing children to make important decisions has serious drawbacks.	*Children can greatly benefit from making important decisions.*

First Supporting Idea

Children do not have the experience and knowledge to make important decisions.

Supporting Example

make decisions about education

Second Supporting Idea

Children fail to think about the long-term effects of their choices.

Supporting Example

college students choosing majors

Conclusion

I contend that parents should make important decisions until their children are young adults.

First Supporting Idea

Children can gain experience by making decisions.

Supporting Example

friend without experience made decisions; made bad decisions

Second Supporting Idea

Important decisions can change the lives of children.

Supporting Example

going abroad to study

Conclusion

I do not think that parents should make important decisions for their children.

Sample Response   p.102

Critical Analysis

1   Ⓑ

2   Ⓐ

3   for one, for example, in contrast

● Chapter | 06 Integrated Writing

Environmental Science: Electric Vehicles vs. Gasoline-Powered Vehicles

Vocabulary   p.104

1   efficient

2   maintenance

3   released

4   repair

5   recharge

6   internal combustion engine

7   mechanic

8   pollutants

9   break down

10   battery

Reading   p.105

Summarizing

Main Idea

The reading passage argues that people have *many good reasons* to buy electric vehicles.

First Supporting Argument

To begin with, the passage explains that electric vehicles are good *for the environment*. The reason is that they produce *no pollutants*. Their batteries are also *energy efficient*. And they are better for the environment than cars that use gas.

Second Supporting Argument

The passage then argues that electric vehicles do not require *much maintenance*. Unlike internal combustion engines, which often break down, the engines of EVs do not. So people do not have to *pay mechanics* to repair their cars.

Vocabulary   p.106

1   inexpensive

2   terrible

3   power plant

4   replacement

5   emissions

6   average

7   requires

8   poison

9   fee

10   mining

Listening   p.107

Script   02-06

M: Now listen to part of a lecture on the topic you just read about.

Professor: I heard there are many reasons to purchase electric vehicles. So I did some research on EVs. Interestingly, I discovered that EVs are not quite as good as people claim.

People say that EVs don't produce any emissions, so they're good for the environment. Yet the process of making an EV creates a great amount of pollution. And the batteries EVs use are made of lithium.

Lithium mining is terrible for the environment. It uses very much water, can poison the land and the water, and releases large amounts of harmful emissions. And let's not forget about recharging EVs. Where do you think the electricity comes from? It's often made in coal-burning power plants. So, no, EVs are not actually good for the environment.

Some people claim that EVs are inexpensive because they require no maintenance. Well, the average price of an EV is about $20,000 more than a gasoline-powered car. If you want a nice EV, you'll have to pay even more. In addition, the batteries sometimes need to be replaced. In most cases, a replacement battery costs at least $15,000. So you might not pay too much in maintenance fees. But EVs are still too expensive for most people.

Summarizing

Main Idea

The lecturer states that EVs are *not as good* as people claim they are.

First Supporting Argument

The lecturer starts by stating that *making EVs* creates pollution. He then adds that *lithium mining* is terrible for the environment and that EVs get recharged with electricity from *coal-burning power plants*.

Second Supporting Argument

Next, the lecturer talks about the prices of EVs. He mentions that they cost around $20,000 more than a *gasoline-powered car*. In addition, it costs at least $15,000 to *replace a battery* on an EV.

▮ Paraphrasing Exercise   p.108

Reading
Answers may vary.

1   *The reading passage argues that buying electric vehicles provides many* advantages *for people.*

2   *To begin with, the passage explains that electric vehicles do not* harm *the environment.*

3   *The reason is that they do not* create *any pollutants.*

4   *The passage then argues that electric vehicles do not need to be* repaired *very often.*

5   *Unlike internal combustion engines, which often* stop *working, the engines of EVs do not.*

Listening
Answers may vary.

1   *The lecturer comments that EVs are* worse *than people say that they are.*

2   *The lecturer begins by stating that* manufacturing *EVs makes pollution.*

3   *He then adds that lithium mining is terrible for the environment and that EVs* utilize *electricity from coal-burning power plants.*

4   *Next, the lecturer talks about how much EVs* cost.

5   *He mentions that they can be around $20,000 more* expensive *than a gasoline-powered car.*

▮ Tandem Note-Taking   p.109
Answers may vary.

Reading	Listening
Main Idea *There are many good reasons to buy electric vehicles.*	**Main Idea** *Electric vehicles are not as good as people claim.*
First Supporting Argument *Electric vehicles are good for the environment.*	**First Supporting Argument** *EVs created pollution in various ways.*
Supporting Detail *produce no pollutants; batteries energy efficient*	Supporting Detail *making EVs creates pollution; lithium mining bad for the environment; EVs recharged by coal-burning power plants*
Second Supporting Argument *Electric vehicles do not need much maintenance.*	**Second Supporting Argument** *EVs are not as cheap as people say they are.*
Supporting Detail *engines do not break down; do not need to pay mechanics for repairs*	Supporting Detail *$20,000 more than gas-powered cars; $15,000 to replace a battery*

▮ Sample Response   p.111

Critical Analysis

1   Ⓐ

2   Ⓐ

3   pricey

4   firstly, in addition, however, finally

Improving Schools Is Most Important for Development

▎ Background & Brainstorming   p.112

Understanding the Background
Answers may vary.

1 improve their schools

2 richest nation

3 Large companies

4 basic industrial services

5 better schools

6 good government policies

7 lower crime rates

8 more money

Selecting Ideas

Agree

- In order for a country to develop, it must improve its schools. *(Topic Sentence)*

- Large companies require workers that are well educated.

- Places with more educated people have less crime.

Disagree

- Improving other factors is more important for the development of a nation. *(Topic Sentence)*

- Intelligent government policies can also result in economic growth.

- Nations must first provide their people with basic industrial services.

Generating Ideas
Answers may vary.

Agree

1 A nation must *improve its schools* in order to become developed.

2 Well-*educated people* are less likely to commit crimes.

3 Large companies need employees that have a *good education*.

Disagree

1 *Other factors* must be improved in order for a nation to develop.

2 A nation with good *government policies* can also grow its economy.

3 People of a nation must have *basic industrial services* first.

▎ Planning   p.114

Answers may vary.

Agree	Disagree
Thesis Statement *I believe that a nation must develop its schools in order to become developed.*	**Thesis Statement** *I feel that other factors must be improved for a nation to develop.*
First Supporting Idea *Large companies need educated workers.*	**First Supporting Idea** *A nation must develop its basic industrial services.*
Supporting Example *develop new technologies; sell to foreign countries*	Supporting Example *roads, sewers, and power plants; needed for other development*
Second Supporting Idea *Nations with more educated people are safer.*	**Second Supporting Idea** *Good government policies can help a country develop.*
Supporting Example *lower crime rates; better quality of life*	Supporting Example *trade and money policies; growth in China*
Conclusion *I hold that a nation cannot develop unless it first improves its schools.*	**Conclusion** *I firmly believe that the development of industry and good government policies are more important for a country to become developed.*

▎ Sample Response   p.116

Critical Analysis

1 Ⓑ

2 Ⓑ

3 additionally, nevertheless

Astronomy: The Benefits of Space Exploration

Vocabulary
p.118

1 bacteria
2 government
3 affect
4 donate
5 exploration
6 addressed
7 volcano
8 advance
9 poverty
10 astounded

Reading
p.119

Summarizing

Main Idea

The writer believes that governments should *focus on the Earth* rather than spend money on space exploration.

First Supporting Argument

First, much of the Earth still has not *been explored*. The text then states that scientists continue to make *new discoveries* all the time.

Second Supporting Argument

There are still *many problems* on the Earth that need to be solved. Instead of spending money on the *International Space Station*, governments should *donate the money* to those in need.

Vocabulary
p.120

1 crowded
2 developments
3 colonization
4 modern
5 key
6 exists
7 The human race
8 brought about

Listening
p.121

Script
02-07

M: Now listen to part of a lecture on the topic you just read about.

Professor: I will tell you more about space exploration today. Our travels into space have brought about some very important developments. And I'm sure that space travel will become even more important in the future. Therefore, we must continue our exploration of outer space.

One key benefit of space exploration relates to colonization. In the future, the Earth will become very crowded. There simply won't be enough room for everybody. Fortunately, space exploration can solve this problem. Going into space teaches us how space affects the human body in the long term. We can also start to build colonies on other planets. We can find out how to live on these planets. So as you can see, space exploration is important for the future of the human race.

Second, many scientific advancements have resulted from space exploration. A lot of modern technology would not exist without it. A great example is computers. Space exploration resulted in the creation of the microchip. This led to the development of the modern personal computer, like the ones some of you are using now. And let's not forget about the research that continues to this day. Without it, our lives would be much less comfortable and enjoyable.

Summarizing

Main Idea

The instructor presents two reasons why we must *continue our exploration* of outer space.

First Supporting Argument

The opening argument deals with *colonization*. The Earth will become very crowded in the future. By traveling into space, we can learn how space affects the *human body* in the long term. We can also start *building colonies* in space.

Second Supporting Argument

There are also the *scientific advancements* that have come from space exploration. Space exploration led to the development of the *modern personal computer*.

Paraphrasing Exercise

p.122

Reading

Answers may vary.

1 The author of the passage feels that governments should <u>concentrate</u> on the Earth instead of spending money on exploring space.

2 To begin with, there are still many things on the Earth to <u>learn about</u>.

3 Consequently, researchers <u>continue</u> to make new discoveries.

4 Additionally, the Earth has several problems that must be <u>fixed</u>.

5 Governments should <u>give money</u> to needy people rather than spend it on space research.

Listening

Answers may vary.

1 In the lecture, the instructor gives two arguments in favor of <u>outer space exploration</u>.

2 The Earth will eventually become <u>overpopulated</u>.

3 Traveling into space <u>can teach</u> us how outer space causes changes in the human body.

4 Several scientific <u>developments</u> have occurred because of space exploration.

5 Space exploration led to the <u>creation</u> of the present personal computers.

Tandem Note-Taking

p.123

Answers may vary.

Reading	Listening
Main Idea	**Main Idea**
The author of the passage feels that governments should concentrate on the Earth.	The speaker feels that we must continue our exploration of space.
First Supporting Argument	**First Supporting Argument**
There are still many things on the Earth to learn about.	The Earth will eventually become completely full.
Supporting Detail	Supporting Detail
recently discovered bacteria that get energy from volcanoes	learn how space causes changes in the human body; start building colonies in space
Second Supporting Argument	**Second Supporting Argument**
The Earth has several problems that must be fixed.	Space exploration has led to many scientific developments.
Supporting Detail	Supporting Detail
governments should donate money to the needy	development of modern personal computer

Sample Response

p.125

Critical Analysis

1 Ⓒ

2 Ⓐ

3 modern

4 first, in fact, on the contrary

● Chapter | 07 Independent Writing

Attending a Live Performance or Watching One on TV

Background & Brainstorming

p.126

Understanding the Background

Answers may vary.

1 Many people feel that going to live performances is more <u>exciting</u>.

2 Seeing a performance with a crowd is a(n) <u>powerful experience</u> for many people.

3 To watch a performance live, you must spend money on <u>tickets and transportation</u>.

4 Attending a performance in person creates a(n) <u>special memory</u>.

5 It is less <u>time consuming</u> to watch a performance on television.

6 At a live performance, you can see the performer <u>up close</u>.

7 Watching a performance on television is <u>more comfortable</u>.

8 You are with <u>other fans</u> at a live performance.

Selecting Ideas

Attend in Person

- Being at a performance in person is superior to watching it on television. *(Topic Sentence)*
- Attending a live performance is a more powerful experience than seeing it on television.
- You can create a long-lasting memory by going to a live performance.

Watch on Television

- It is better to watch a performance on television. (Topic Sentence)
- Seeing a performance on television is less expensive.
- Watching a performance on television takes much less time than going in person.

Generating Ideas

Answers may vary.

Attend in Person

1 It is *more enjoyable* to be at a performance in person than to watch it on television.

2 Being at a live show is *more exciting* than seeing it on television.

3 Attending a live performance can create a *long-lasting memory*.

Watch on Television

1 Seeing a performance *on television* is better than watching it in person.

2 Watching a performance on television is *less expensive*.

3 Going to a performance takes *a lot of time*.

▮ Planning
p.128

Answers may vary.

Attend in Person	Watch on Television
Thesis Statement	**Thesis Statement**
I would much rather attend a live performance in person.	*I prefer watching a performance on television.*
First Supporting Idea	**First Supporting Idea**
Being at a live show is more exciting.	*Watching a live performance on television is less expensive.*

Supporting Example	Supporting Example
can see a performer in person	*save money on tickets and transportation*
Second Supporting Idea	**Second Supporting Idea**
Attending a live performance can create a long-lasting memory.	*Going to a live performance takes a lot of time.*
Supporting Example	**Supporting Example**
have fun with friends	*only spend time watching the performance*
Conclusion	**Conclusion**
Seeing a live performance in person is much more exciting than simply watching it on television.	*I find it more enjoyable to watch a live performance on television.*

▮ Sample Response
p.130

Critical Analysis

1 (B)

2 (A)

3 on top of this, in short

● Chapter | 08 Integrated Writing

Ecology: Using Solar Energy Rather than Fossil Fuels

Vocabulary
p.132

1 pollution

2 traditional energy sources

3 constantly

4 solution

5 poison

6 alternative energy sources

7 forever

8 panel

9 gas

Reading

Summarizing

Main Idea

The reading says that solar energy is the *perfect solution* for the world's energy problems.

First Supporting Argument

The first benefit of solar energy is that it is *environmentally friendly*. Solar energy works by using *special panels* to collect the sun's energy. This happens without *causing pollution*.

Second Supporting Argument

An additional advantage of solar energy is its *low cost*. Solar energy uses the *sun's energy* and solar panels. These make it possible to use the sun's energy forever *at no cost*.

Vocabulary

1 supplement
2 afford
3 maintenance
4 replace
5 fee
6 average
7 hidden cost
8 efficient
9 sensitive
10 drawback

Listing

Listening

Script

M: Now listen to part of a lecture on the topic you just read about.

Professor: A lot of people talk about how great solar energy is. Of course, solar energy has its good points, but it has its share of drawbacks, too.

Environmentalists argue that solar energy can completely replace traditional energy sources. The truth is that it can't. Here. Let me explain why. An average solar panel is about ten to fifteen percent efficient. But do you know what? Coal plants are more than thirty percent efficient. This is a huge difference. There's also the fact that solar energy doesn't work at night or on cloudy days. Do you see what I'm getting at? We can use solar energy to supplement our current energy sources. But we cannot use it to replace them.

Then, there are the hidden costs of solar energy. The sun's energy may be free. But the technology to collect this energy is not. Do you know how much a solar panel costs? This may astound you, but just one panel can cost tens of thousands of dollars. This makes solar energy too expensive for most people to afford. And let's not forget the high maintenance fees of solar panels. They are sensitive pieces of equipment, and they are very expensive to repair.

Summarizing

Main Idea

The lecturer outlines some of *the drawbacks* of solar energy. The lecturer supports his opinion with two examples.

First Supporting Argument

For his first argument, the lecturer states that solar energy cannot replace *traditional energy sources*. The reason is that solar panels are *less efficient* than energy sources such as coal.

Second Supporting Argument

The next reason the lecturer mentions is the *hidden costs* of solar energy. He explains that solar energy panels are too expensive for most people *to afford*. He also says that they have high *maintenance fees*.

Paraphrasing Exercise

Reading

Answers may vary.

1 *The passage claims that the best answer to our energy problems is solar power.*

2 *One advantage of solar energy is that it is good for the environment.*

3 *Solar energy uses special panels to gather the sun's energy.*

4 *Another benefit of solar energy is that it is not expensive.*

5 *The panels allow us to use solar energy endlessly free of charge.*

Listening

Answers may vary.

1 The lecturer talks about some of the <u>disadvantages</u> of solar energy.

2 The first argument given by the lecturer is that solar energy cannot <u>take the place of</u> traditional sources of energy.

3 The lecturer also <u>believes</u> that solar energy has hidden costs.

4 He states that few people are able <u>to buy</u> solar energy panels.

5 The lecturer also mentions that the panels have high <u>repair costs.</u>

▌ Tandem Note-Taking   p.137

Answers may vary.

Reading	Listening
Main Idea	**Main Idea**
The passage claims that the best answer to our energy problems is solar power.	The instructor talks about some of the disadvantages of solar energy.
First Supporting Argument	**First Supporting Argument**
One advantage of solar energy is that it is good for the environment.	Solar energy cannot take the place of traditional energy sources.
Supporting Detail	Supporting Detail
uses special panels to gather the sun's energy; does not cause pollution	solar panels are less efficient than coal
Second Supporting Argument	**Second Supporting Argument**
Another benefit of solar energy is that it is not expensive.	Solar energy has hidden costs.
Supporting Detail	Supporting Detail
able to use solar energy endlessly free of charge	few people able to buy solar panels; have high repair costs

▌ Sample Response   p.139

Critical Analysis

1 Ⓒ

2 Ⓑ

3 supplement

4 to explain why, because of this, at the same time

● Chapter | 08 Independent Writing

It Is Better to Save Money than to Spend It

▌ Background & Brainstorming   p.140

Understanding the Background

Answers may vary.

1 Saving money now allows you to have *more money* later.

2 Spending just *a little money* will make you happier now.

3 The money in a savings account will earn interest and *increase in value*.

4 It is possible to buy a nice car or a(n) *bigger house* if you save your money.

5 You can spend money to make other people *happy*.

6 Saving money also allows you to *retire* when you are not that old.

7 You should also spend money because you never know *what will happen* in the future.

8 Taking your family *on vacation* will make them happier than putting money in a savings account.

Selecting Ideas

Agree

- It is important to save as much money as possible. *(Topic Sentence)*
- Saving money is necessary to retire at a younger age.
- You can make large purchases that improve your life by saving money.

Disagree

- Spending money is preferable to saving money. *(Topic Sentence)*
- It is not possible to know the future, so it is better to spend your money.
- Spending money can make other people happy.

Generating Ideas

Answers may vary.

Agree

1 You should save as *much money* as possible.

2 Making *large purchases* can make your life better.

3 To finish working sooner, you must *save money*.

Disagree

1 It is better to *spend money* than to save it.

2 Other people can be *made happier* if you spend money.

3 You do not know what will happen *in the future*.

▌ Planning   p.142

Answers may vary.

Agree	Disagree
Thesis Statement	**Thesis Statement**
I feel that saving money is preferable to spending it.	*I believe that it is better to spend money than to save it.*
First Supporting Idea	**First Supporting Idea**
Saving money allows you to improve your life.	*Other people can be made happier if you spend money.*
Supporting Example	Supporting Example
buy a larger house	*take family on vacation*
Second Supporting Idea	**Second Supporting Idea**
Saving money also allows you to retire sooner.	*You do not know what will happen in the future.*
Supporting Example	Supporting Example
mother's parents did not save; father's parents saved; stopped working at a young age	*may win lottery; receive money from a relative*
Conclusion	**Conclusion**
I strongly believe that saving money is much better than spending it.	*Spending money is far better than saving it.*

▌ Sample Response   p.144

Critical Analysis

1 Ⓒ

2 Ⓒ

3 first of all, for example, at the same time

Part C

Task 1

Listening

Script   03-03

M: Now listen to part of a lecture on the topic you just read about.

Professor: I enjoy spending time near the water. Sometimes at a lake, I see a fish jump out of the water. Have you ever wondered why fish do that? There are some theories, but each has problems.

Some biologists claim that fish leap out of the water to escape predators. Now, I'm sure this happens. But it can't be the main reason. Let me explain. My uncle has a pond stocked with various types of fish, but none is a predator. By that, I mean they don't eat other fish. Yet whenever I go there, I see fish leaping from the water. Those fish are clearly not trying to escape predators. After all, the pond doesn't have any.

I've also seen a claim that fish leap out of the water to get air. Again, let me discuss my uncle's pond. Occasionally in summertime, the temperature gets hot, and lots of algae grow. The pond's oxygen level decreases very much, and some fish die. But they don't leap out of the water at all. Instead, they die in the water and then float to the surface. That's the only thing that happens to them.

• Model Answer

Both the reading passage and the lecture discuss reasons that fish leap out of the water. The author of the reading passage provides two theories on why fish do that. However, the professor casts doubt on each of those points.

First, the lecturer discusses her uncle's pond. She mentions that it is stocked with fish that do not eat other fish. She points out that the fish in the pond often leap from the water. She says that those fish cannot be trying to escape from predators because the pond has none. The lecturer's comments cast doubt on the point made in the reading passage. It claims that fish leap out of the water to escape from sudden attacks by predators.

Second, the lecturer remarks that her uncle's pond sometimes gets lots of algae. When that happens, some fish die. The fish do not jump out of the water though. Instead, they float to the surface and die. This refutes the argument in the reading passage. According to it, fish like the snakehead and an African catfish can breathe air. So they leap out of the water to get air when there is little oxygen in the water.

Task 2

• Model Answer

Many people living in cities cannot afford to buy cars. Instead, they use public buses and subways as their main methods of transportation. These people would certainly benefit from free public transportation. Even so, I am of the opinion that public transportation should not be made free.

For one, charging for public transportation helps keep it in good condition. In some cities, millions of people use public transportation systems. This causes a lot of wear and tear on the buses and the subway trains. Keeping them in good working order is expensive and takes a lot of time. If public transportation became free, then a lot more people would use public transportation. This would require the buses and the trains to be repaired a lot more often. It would also result in more damage. This would happen because people who do not need to use public transportation would use it and then cause additional damage. In order to keep public transportation systems working properly, there must be a fee.

Even if public transportation became free to use, it would still cost money. A large part of public transportation is paid for by taxes. Making public transportation free would require governments to raise taxes to help cover the cost of the transportation systems. This means that everybody would have to pay for public transportation even if they do not use it. Under the current system, however, people who use public transportation have to pay more to use it. This system is fairer. It is better to charge those who use public transportation than to charge everybody.

To summarize, getting rid of public transportation fees is not a good idea. It would result in more damage to the systems. It would also require people who do not use public transportation to pay more for it.

Task 1

Listening

Script   03-07

M: Now listen to part of a lecture on the topic you just read about.

Professor: You know, it's popular for companies to expand nowadays. But it's not always the best option. Let me give you a couple of reasons why.

First of all, the competition becomes much greater the bigger you get. Imagine a smartphone company trying to compete with Apple. Or think about a company competing with Amazon. Big firms tend to ignore small ones. Those businesses are not threats to them. But as companies expand, they attract attention from the biggest firms. Those firms don't want any competition. So they do their best to make any firms that are expanding fail.

A second point is that quality control may become a problem as a company becomes bigger. Think about it like this. A small company may focus on just one or two products. As it expands, it starts making a wider variety of products. Its best employees can't work on every product though. So it's naturally going to produce inferior products. In other words, there will be less quality control. When quality becomes a problem, a company's reputation suffers. And that can cause big problems for any business.

• Model Answer

The reading passage and the lecturer both address the expansion of companies. The reading passage claims that expansion can have positive results for a company. The lecturer argues that this is not always true.

The lecturer begins by mentioning that the competition is much greater for large companies. He states that big companies have to compete with businesses like Apple and Amazon. Those large companies will make newcomers try to fail. But they will mostly not pay attention to smaller companies. This goes against the argument in the reading passage. It claims that bigger companies have less competition. As a result, they get more revenues and increased profits.

Next, the lecturer talks about problems with quality control at firms that expand. According to the lecturer, when companies expand, their best workers cannot monitor all of their new products. This results in a loss of quality control, so they make inferior products. That means a company's reputation will decrease. This is in contrast to the argument in the reading passage. The author of it argues that when a company expands, it can make and sell more products. This will let it profit more.

Task 2

• Model Answer

Some people believe that parents should teach their children basic economic skills. But I disagree with them. In my opinion, schools need to teach students basic economic skills. I feel this way for a couple of reasons.

To begin with, too many young people lack basic economic skills. For example, they do not understand concepts such as supply and demand. They also do not know much about interest payments. As a result, they can have problems when they get credit cards. This happened to my sister. She got a credit card and used it too much. So she had a lot of debt. Even worse, she did not understand why that happened. She had to work two jobs to make enough money to pay back all of her debts. She could have used a basic economics class at school. She could have learned how to use money properly. Then, she would not have had such a big problem.

Furthermore, teachers know how to instruct their students well. My teachers at school are excellent instructors. They can explain difficult topics easily. This is especially true of my math teacher. He can make difficult math problems easy to solve. Math is important to economics. So I believe he would be good at teaching basic economic skills. Teachers at schools also have access to learning tools. They can use computer programs to teach students about economics. By using computers, teachers can make lessons fun and easy for their students. This means that their students will enjoy learning about economics.

In conclusion, young people do not have enough basic economic skills. Teachers also have the ability to instruct students well. For those two reasons, I believe that schools need to teach students basic economic skills.

MEMO

MEMO

TOEFL®
MAP
New TOEFL® Edition

Writing

Basic